Reverent Rituals

Reverent Rituals

✦

A Brief Wedding Guide

New and Revised Edition

Rev. Dr. Russell K. Elleven

iUniverse, Inc.

New York Lincoln Shanghai

Reverent Rituals
A Brief Wedding Guide

iUniverse, Inc.

For information address:
iUniverse, Inc.
2021 Pine Lake Road, Suite 100
Lincoln, NE 68512
www.iuniverse.com

ISBN: 0-595-29807-9

Printed in the United States of America

For Gayle

"Perfect love is rare indeed—
for to be a lover will require that you continually
have the subtlety of the very wise,
the flexibility of the child, the sensitivity of the artist,
the understanding of the philosopher, the acceptance of the saint,
the tolerance of the scholar and the fortitude of the certain."
—Leo Buscaglia

Contents

1

An Introduction

o o o o o o o o o o o o o o o o o o o o o o o o o o o o o o o o o o
Time is too slow for those who wait,
too swift for those who fear,
too long for those who grieve,
too short for those who rejoice,
but for those who love, time is eternity.

—Henry Van Dyke

The couple was young and in love. These two people had their whole lives in front of them and wanted to spend that time together as husband and wife. I could see their excitement, feel their anticipation, and understand their need to do this the "right" way.

Craig and Jenny did not have a minister to perform their ceremony. They were not a regular member of a religious community but did not want to get married on the steps of the local courthouse. They asked if I could help. The answer, of course, was a resounding yes!

As I began to know Craig and Jenny better I saw their excitement fade. The wedding was becoming more a chore rather than a celebration. They just wanted this to all be over. Everyone was telling them what to do and how to do it. Jenny and Craig had become overwhelmed by it all and wondered, as do many couples, if this was all worth the trouble. What a disappointing way to begin their new lives in marriage.

What happened to Craig and Jenny occurs time and again. The couple allowed the wedding planning to become bigger than the marriage itself. The tasks, the traditions, the relatives, all with wonderful intentions, made the wedding a burden. The couple had ceded its powers of choice to others. The wedding did not feel like it was theirs anymore. Jenny's tears of happiness had turned into tears of pain.

This little book is meant for couples like Jenny and Craig who are intending to get married and who are planning their own wedding ceremony. Thankfully there have been many changes in the roles of women and men in today's society. However, it is still the case that most often it is the bride who does the majority of the planning for a wedding. I hope couples who read this book will do so together.

If you are the bride reading this book my hope is that you will extend an invitation to your future husband to take part in the planning of your wedding. If you are the groom reading this book I offer you my congratulations. Many times men will assume the woman will do all of the work and planning. Men often believe they must merely show up and be present for the ceremony. This should no longer be the case in the 21st century.

The wedding is your special day as a couple. It should reflect *your* beliefs and attitudes of marriage in order to be real for both of you. If not, it is merely a ritualized event that holds little meaning and does not speak to your beliefs and life circumstance. Together, you can make this event special and different from all others.

There is much to do. There is much to plan. There are traditions the two of you may want to incorporate into your wedding. There are other traditions you may want to delete altogether as they do not fit with the way you view yourself as an individual or as a couple. Weddings can be complicated events but they do not have to be. There are many resources available to make your wedding easier to plan.

For many couples today a wedding consultant may be the best answer. The consultant can take the worry out of your wedding by assisting in the creation of a wedding budget, suggesting through a network of vendors who will give wonderful service within your budgetary requirements, and oversee the rehearsal, ceremony, and reception. However, there is also a great deal of pride that comes from creating this ever-so-important event together as a couple. This may be your first opportunity to work on a large project together. This will be a wonderful opportunity to work together and make your dream wedding come true.

There may be many things that you, as a couple, believe should be a part of or incorporated into a wedding ceremony. I encourage you to do those things. Women, more often than men, have played out their wedding in their minds long before Mr. Right came along. Do those things that have formed your dream wedding in your mind. If certain words were spoken in the ceremony-use those words. If certain phrases were omitted from your ceremony—omit those words. If specific rituals within the ceremony were performed—perform those rituals. You know what you want and have the opportunity to be creative. Your wedding date is an opportunity to help that dream become a reality.

One theme you will hear throughout this little book is to make this *your* event. Take the advice of others, including what is contained in this book, and measure it carefully. You will probably know internally if the advice is right for your wedding. Wedding traditions, mothers, and many others will pretend to know what you should do in your wedding. You may want to decide right now that this is your wedding and the two of you will dictate how the wedding looks, feels, sounds and even smells.

How this Book Came About

This book was first written in 2002 under the title, *A Brief Wedding Guide to Reverent Rituals: Setting the Stage for the Perfect Ceremony* published by Writer's Club Press. In this updated edition I have added a few things, deleted others, and hope you will find a book that is easily and quickly read and one that offers you traditional and alternative ways to think of your wedding.

This book is arranged to help you make informed wedding ceremony decisions. Together we will examine a few wedding traditions, how to choose the person to perform the ceremony, premarital counseling and a host of other things. Be advised that most chapters you will read could be complete books themselves. I have attempted to greatly condense the information in a way that does not become onerous to the reader. If nothing else, I hope this book will serve as a catalyst to your wedding planning. Should you desire to do further, more in-depth research, I have provided both book and Internet resources at the end of the final chapter.

I have had the privilege in assisting hundreds of couples create their wedding ceremonies. I have looked into their eyes as they promise to have and to hold one another throughout eternity. I have laughed with them and cried with them as they took this bold step into the future as husband and wife. I believe what is in this little book would have been helpful to Craig and Jenny. I hope what you read will prove helpful to you.

Again, if you take nothing else from this book, please do understand that you have the power and ability to shape your wedding into whatever you want it to be. You have choices. I wish you all the best as you begin this endeavor together.

2

Before You Get Started: Financial Matters

o o o o o o o o o o o o o o o o o o o o o o o o o o o o o o o o

In the arithmetic of love,
one plus one equals everything,
and two minus one equals nothing.

—Mignon McLaughlin

Jeff and Denise felt sick to their stomachs. They had planned a tremendously lavish wedding and had recently found out Denise's parents had no intention of paying for the production. The couple was trying to decide what should be done and having a terrible time trying to decide what to cut out of the wedding budget. They were also disagreeing quite a bit with one another as to what was most important for this very special day.

Jeff and Denise's situation is all too common. There will be over two million weddings this year. According to CNN, the average wedding runs over $22,000. I am by no means a financial expert but I do know this is a great deal of money. And, as more and more couples are marrying later in life, they are shouldering the vast majority of the wedding costs.

I believe it important for the two of you to have a serious conversation about the amount of money you are willing to spend on the wedding. In working with couples I have found it easiest to start with a specific dollar figure and then build your budget around that amount.

The table below may prove helpful in sorting out your expenses. It allows you to take the amount of money intended for the wedding and roughly estimate the percentage of dollars distributed among several categories.

Sample Wedding Expenses

Attire		**19%**
Bride	9.0	
Bride's Attendants	7.5	
Groom & Attendants	2.5	
Ceremony		**4.5**
Site	3.5	
Music	1.0	
Flowers		5.0
Misc.		4.5
Photographer/Videographer		9.0
Reception		44.5
Rings		13.5
Total		**100%**

For arguments sake, let's say the two of you desire to spend no more than $15,000 for your wedding. Given the percentages in the sample above, your budget might then look like this:

Your Wedding Budget

Bride's Attire	1350.00
Bride's Attendants	1125.00
Groom & Attendants	375.00
Ceremony Site	525.00
Ceremony Music	150.00
Flowers	750.00
Misc.	675.00
Photographer/Videographer	1350.00
Reception	6675.00
Rings	2025.00
Total	**$15,000.00**

You might see from this example that some amounts seem very low for what you have in mind. Other amounts in this sample budget may seem extraordinarily high to you both. At the very least, this exercise can get the two of you talking about the very real expense of your wedding and avoid the problems many couples confront when figuring the bottom line of the nuptials. Talking about these financial issues now will probably save hurt feelings and damaged pocketbooks in the future.

Cost Saving Tips

There are a few things you can do right away in order to alleviate some of the hefty wedding price tag. First, try to have your wedding and reception in the same location. Often this strategy will lead to significant savings. An added benefit is that your guests then do not have to travel, and possibly get lost, from wedding to reception site.

Second, have a cash bar rather than paying for your guests alcoholic beverages. You will save even more money if you have no alcoholic beverage service at all.

Some couples compromise and pay for a certain kind of alcoholic beverage. For example, you may choose to pay for wine but not beer or liquor. Or, you may choose to pay for the first two drinks for your guests.

Third, be willing to shop around. You will probably find a variety of fee schedules during your wedding vendor search. For instance, an up-and-coming wedding photographer new to the business will likely charge less than an established professional. While you may often get what you pay for, there may be times when you agree to take a risk with a less experienced vendor.

Also, come to my wedding website (www.wedding-ceremony.com) and click on the "Bookstore" icon. There are several good books that will assist you in finding bridal bargains.

Just in Case

It may be this talk of price shopping bores you because you know your family will definitely pay for the wedding of your dreams. If that is the case, it may be that you are more interested in who traditionally pays for what in the wedding scenario. Take a look at the following:

The bride pays for:

- Bridegroom's wedding ring

- Her hair stylist and make-up artist

- Housing for out-of-town guests

- Presents for her attendants

- Stationary for personal notes and thank-you notes

- Wedding gift for the groom

- Wedding guest book and other accessories she wants

The bride's family pays for:

- Aisle carpet and/or canopy

- Bouquets or corsages for bridesmaids, honor attendants, and flower girl

- Bride's wedding clothes and trousseau

- Their own attire

- Rental fees for ceremony site

- Fees for organist, soloist, or other musical accompaniment

- Engagement and wedding photographs

- Engagement party

- Entire cost of the reception

- Flowers for ceremony and reception

- Invitations, announcements, enclosures and mailing costs

- Transportation for bridal party from house to ceremony to reception

- Their wedding gift to the couple

   The bride and/or her family pays for:

- Services of a wedding consultant

- Boutonniere for the fathers and grandfathers

- Security arrangements for gifts at home

- Traffic policeman

- A party for the bridesmaids, if no one else pays for it

   The groom pays for:

- His wedding attire

- Boutonnieres for his attendants and himself

- Bride's bouquet

- Corsage for the bride's going-away outfit

- Corsages for any female honored guest, such as grandmothers or godmothers

- Fee for the clergy or officiant

- Flowers for both mothers

- Gift for the bride

- Gloves, ascots or ties for his attendants if they are purchased, not rented

- Bride's wedding and engagement rings

- Honeymoon

- Housing for his out-of-town attendants

- Marriage license

- Shipping for wedding presents

- Bachelor party if no one else pays for it

    The groom's family pays for:

- Rehearsal dinner

- Their clothes for the wedding

- Travel and accommodations for themselves

- Wedding gift for the couple

- Any other costs, as decided

    The ushers pay for:

- An individual gift for the couple or a contribution of a gift from all the ushers

- Rental of wedding outfit

- Travel expenses

- Bachelor party

The bridesmaids pay for:

- An individual gift for the couple or a contribution to a gift from all the brides-maids

- Purchase of bridesmaid's dresses and accessories

- Shower and/or luncheon for the bride

- Travel expenses

The out-of-town guests pay for:

- Transportation and lodging

- Gift for the couple

Regardless of whoever pays for the wedding, I believe it important for the two of you to have a conversation about your wedding budget. Do not take it for granted that mother or father will pay for anything. Talk to them first. Do not take it for granted that you both have the same taste in flowers. Talk about it together. Do not take for granted that you both have the same level of comfort with running up credit card debt. Talk to each other about plastic debt.

My hope is these messages continue on in your marriage. Do not take each other for granted. Talk about your differences.

3

Why We Do What We Do: Wedding Traditions

o o o o o o o o o o o o o o o o o o o o o o o o o o o o o o o o o o o o

And now here is my secret, a very simple secret;
it is only with the heart that one can see rightly,
what is essential is invisible to the eye.

—Antoine de Saint-Exupery

David and Julie were all decked out in their wedding attire. Her dress was magnificent and she looked beautiful. He was a little uncomfortable but figured he could stay in his tuxedo jacket until the first dance was completed. All of the attendants were dressed in colors the bride had chosen. Their photographs were beautiful and they were often complimented on their wedding day of how wonderful everything looked.

Their friends, Jerry and Mickey, decided to be married at the beach. They were both drawn to the water, were certified as SCUBA divers, and planned many of their future vacations to be around water. She wore a simple white flowing sun dress. He wore white linen pants and a shirt. They were both barefoot as they looked into one another's eyes to say their vows. Everything was splendid.

Both couples had the wedding they wanted. One wedding is viewed to be more traditional than the other. Traditions are often what ground us as a society or a culture. Traditions can be very powerful and hold great meaning for people. At the same time, some traditions may have outlived their usefulness. At one time it was a ceremony tradition that wives should, "Love, honor, and OBEY" their husbands. I have never officiated a wedding in which the wife was required by the wedding vows to obey her husband. It appears that tradition is no longer desirous for most couples.

Yet it does cause one to wonder about wedding traditions. Have you ever wondered why we do the things we do at weddings? Weddings are steeped in tradition. Yes, traditions are good in that they ground us to our past. Traditions often will help us make meaning out of our future. At the same time, traditions can often keep us stuck in the past and not allow us to proceed in important aspects of our lives. The two of you must decide how much tradition will play a part in your wedding.

Many women today are no longer being "given away" at the altar. This tradition stems from the time when women were seen more as property than as a living, loving, contributing partner in a marriage. The dowry of a bride was basically the financial package fathers put together to offer the husband-to-be. The larger the dowry, the better husband a father could attract for his daughter (and the bigger the father's prestige).

So, traditionally, when I ask "Who gives this woman in marriage?" and the father responds, "I do." we are reliving a time when fathers had absolute authority to offer their daughters in marriage. Many women now request their father to say, "We do," or "Her family and I do" as a way around this predicament. Some people also believe the tradition of lifting the bride's veil at the close of the ceremony symbolizes the women now becoming property of the husband. You may, or may not, want to incorporate these traditions into your wedding.

This chapter provides only a cursory glance at wedding traditions. If you are very interested in wedding traditions I would suggest the book entitled, *A Bride's Book of Wedding Traditions* by Arlene Hamilton Stewart. Much of what I present here comes from that excellent book.

The Ceremony

As a minister, I believe the ceremony to be the most important ritual of the wedding day. Today, couples speak to one another of their love and hope for their future together within the ceremony. There is, of course, an entire chapter of this book devoted to the marriage ceremony with numerous examples. But presented here are just a few things you might not have known about wedding ceremony traditions.

One item of interest is that the procession is a remnant of time when brides needed to be protected from harm as they traveled to their wedding. There were plenty of things that might preclude the bride from attending her own wedding. Natural occurrences such as weather elements and also those times when someone (or some group) did not agree the wedding should take place or who might try to keep the bride from her ceremony.

Weddings could even become somewhat dangerous endeavors. Women were sometimes physically taken from a family and forced to marry her abductor. For this reason, brides stand on the left-hand side of a groom during the ceremony. Because most people are right handed, the groom was able to reach his sword if necessary to protect his bride.

The Best Man was originally the partner of the groom who assisted in capturing the bride if necessary. He then stood by his friend during the ceremony to protect the bride and groom if any trouble were to begin. Even today, the Best Man probably has the largest single role in the wedding. Refer to chapter six for all of the Best Man duties.

The Dress

Oh, that beautiful wedding dress. It is the one you have dreamed of, read about, and wished for all of your life. The bride is dressed all in white as pure as the driven snow. Today we take the color of the dress quite for granted. But white was not always the color of choice.

Wedding dresses have an incredibly interesting history. Women used to dress in a wide variety of colors for their wedding. All colors were acceptable. In fact, women usually just wore the best dress they owned for their wedding. The idea of wearing a dress one time was a bit preposterous in the olden days.

The idea of a white wedding gown did not grow in popularity until the year 1840. That is the year Queen Victoria of England was married. Her gown was beautiful and the newspapers raved of Victoria's beauty that day. This is amazing in and of itself because Victoria was not known as a beautiful woman!

The idea that a woman could be a beautiful queen for a day was very appealing to the masses. The women began to dress as their queen did for her wedding. The train of a dress also is a semblance of the wedding dress' royal history. The tiara is a sort of small crown befitting of royalty. The tradition continues to this day although we do see a few wonderful exceptions from time to time.

Colors

Colors were very meaningful for weddings at one time. An old English rhyme has stayed with us that explain wedding colors. It reads:

> *Married in white, you have chosen right,*
> *Married in gray, you will go far away,*
> *Married in black, you will wish yourself back,*
> *Married in red, you will wish yourself dead,*
> *Married in green, ashamed to be seen,*
> *Married in blue, he will always be true,*
> *Married in pearl, you will live in a whirl,*
> *Married in yellow, ashamed of your fellow,*
> *Married in brown, you will live out of town,*
> *Married in pink, your spirit will sink.*

The Victorians also had a language of flowers. Flowers were, and still are today, used to bring a great deal of color into the wedding ceremony. For the Victorians, color, length of stem, and whether or not thorns were present or removed from roses all meant important things.

The Victorians assigned particular flowers to each month. There were:

January—Snowdrop

February—Primrose

March—Jonquil

April—Sweet Pea

May—Lily of the Valley

June—Rose

July—Larkspur

August—Poppy

September—Morning Glory

October—Cosmos

November—Chrysanthemum

December—Holly

Something Old, Something New, Something Borrowed, Something Blue, and a Silver Sixpence in Her Shoe.

Even though some today consider it superstitious, this wedding tradition is very fun. Brides will still try to get these items into their attire for the big day. This combination is supposed to bring to the couple's marriage good luck.

"Something Old" represents the link with the bride's family and the past. Many brides will wear a piece of antique family jewelry or sometimes her mother's wedding gown. Others may choose the family Bible for this part of the ceremony so as to include something old.

"Something New" represents good fortune and success and her hopes for a bright future in her new life. Most often, the wedding gown is the new item. It could also be a special piece of lingerie or a gift the groom has given the bride.

"Something Borrowed" is to remind the bride that friends and family will be there for her when help is needed. Borrowing something from a happily married friend is often most appropriate. The hope is to lend the bride some of her own marital happiness to bring into the new union. Sometimes a friend's veil is used.

"Something Blue" is the symbol of faithfulness and loyalty. Often the blue item is the garter. Biblical Hebrews wore blue ribbons on the border of their wedding clothes to signify love, modesty and fidelity. Blue is also associated with the Virgin Mary. Topaz earrings are sometimes worn to meet this requirement.

"A Silver Sixpence in her Shoe" is to wish the bride future wealth. The shoe is a symbol of authority. Some brides still place a penny in their shoe during the marriage ceremony (although a dime would probably be more true to the saying).

Have fun with this tradition if you choose to incorporate it into your day. It can be joyous and sentimental when choosing the items for your big day.

Tying the Knot

Some believe the expression "tying the knot" dates back to the times of Rome when the bride wore a girdle secured by a knot. On the wedding night, the groom then had the honors of "untying the knot." The couple's lives were then tied together.

Others trace the origin back to Denmark where couples bound themselves to one another. They literally tied a knot in the rope or twine they used in the ceremony. For much of history the rope was the most powerful way to connect things and people. Many trace this back to a ritual called handfasting in which the couple has its hands tied together. We still see this performed in some weddings today with a medieval theme.

Don't Like it—Don't Do it

Wedding traditions are fun to acknowledge and to sometimes incorporate into your wedding. However, some traditions may not speak to your understanding of equality or property. What you do should be reflective of your values and beliefs. Do not let tradition or family expectations pressure you into something that does not feel right.

Again, remember, this is your wedding, no one else's. The only things you must do are proscribed by the state, certain religions, or denominations. In many states, for example, in accordance to law the couple must be asked whether or not the two individuals want to be joined in marriage. We typically accomplish this for through the "I dos." As far as many states are concerned, everything else we do in the ceremony is simply because of the couple's desires or religious requirements.

A religion may also have certain requirements that must be met in order for the ceremony to be valid. Likewise, some Christian denominations have different expectations that must be met in order to be valid. Some of these might come in the form of a specific text that must be used, a specific place the wedding must be held, or specific words that must be uttered in order for the marriage to be recognized by that faith tradition.

If your circumstance does not have any of these requirements you are then free to do what holds the most meaning to you as a couple. You should put great thought into your options and make this wedding as special as it can be for the two of you. Sometimes traditions will play a role in making your wedding special. Sometimes, new traditions must be created in order for the two people to be true and honest with their own outlook of life.

4

Who Will Perform Your Ceremony: Choosing the Officiant

○ ○
"Love is friendship set to music."

—*E. Joseph Crossmann*

Theda and James had just attended a wedding of a mutual friend. Many months after the wedding, Theda asked her friend about the ceremony. In her mind the minister had "gone off on a tangent" and practically held an alter call in the middle of the ceremony. Theda knew her friend was not particularly religious and wondered what had happened.

The friend was a little bit embarrassed about the entire event. She had no idea the minister was going to give a sermon in the middle of her wedding. She would never have consented to allowing this had she known it was coming. When Theda spoke to me about officiating her wedding she wanted to make sure I would not be giving a sermon. She did not want to be embarrassed as her friend had been.

The person you choose to officiate your ceremony will have a lasting impact on your wedding memories. Because of this, it is crucial that you interview prospective officiants carefully to make sure you are in one accord with your wedding wishes and requirements.

Of course, if you are part of a religious community you will most likely use your minister or religious leader to perform the ceremony. However, many couples do not have a church home but wish to have more of a ceremony than can be offered on the courthouse steps or in the office of a Justice of the Peace. It does not have to be that way at all if you want something more. By the same token, a courthouse wedding may be all that you want, although I would not think you would be reading this book.

Again, if you do have a church home it is best to ask your pastor to perform the ceremony. But there may also be circumstances where you may be forced to choose another ceremony officiant. For instance, if your minister is out of town the weekend you choose to marry, you have just moved to a new community and have not yet found the religious community that best suits your needs, or if you are not fond of the minister you have and desire to be married outside of the church where you worship you may need to make alternative arrangements for someone to officiate your wedding.

There are many ministers who are willing and able to give you more than the courthouse wedding described above. These ministers greatly enjoy assisting couples write their ceremony and helping wedding dreams come true. Couples should also be careful consumers in choosing the person who will preside over their nuptials. Ministers are, in some ways, similar to any other vendor who will help you on the special day. Yet at the same time there are also major differences from other vendors.

For example, if the vendor you choose to serve as entertainment (i.e. band or disc jockey) for your reception does not show up—you can still get married. It is also indeed tragic if the bakery you choose for your wedding cake forgets your wedding date. You can, however, still get married without a wedding cake. The same cannot be said for the person performing the ceremony.

The person who presides over your wedding ceremony is not like any of these other vendors. Simply stated, you cannot get married if the officiant does not show up for your wedding. I must admit to being a bit biased on this matter because this is how I help couples. It is worth stating that while your officiant is someone you may "employ" for a short period of time, he or she should not be treated as one of the hired hands.

A bit of research with your state or county might be appropriate in order to find out who can legally preside over a wedding ceremony. The first step you might consider is contacting the institution that administers and processes the marriage licenses in your area. Most often this will be the county courthouse. Ask the clerk who your state allows to perform wedding ceremonies. You will probably be given a list of officials who may solemnize your vows. It may be that judges, ministers, or even Notary Publics may perform weddings in your area. Write down each category so you can make certain the person you choose to perform the ceremony fits into your state's guidelines.

Some states require the minister to be licensed or registered with the appropriate authorities. Other states have virtually no restrictions regarding who may preside over a wedding. Be prepared by making sure you know who can (or cannot) perform weddings in your area. This knowledge will help you in finding the right person to pronounce you husband and wife.

Where Do I Find An Officiant?

Locating the person who will preside over the ceremony may be easier than you think. If using a bridal consultant, she or he is very likely to have worked with a number of officiants and can make recommendations to you. If your wedding consultant is unable to recommend an officiant or you are not using a wedding consultant you still have several viable options.

If the location of your wedding is popular among couples they will almost always have someone they can recommend. You may even be provided with a list of prospective wedding ministers. Some locations will only allow you to use their officiant. This is great if you like the person and you will have one more piece of your wedding puzzle completed.

If you do not click with the person you might look at other options either with your chosen location or by searching for a more flexible facility. Be delicate with your questions if the facility requires you to use their officiant. Many times the officiant is the spouse or a very close friend of the person to whom you are speaking. In my experience it is true that in some facilities the coordinator of the wedding location or chapel may also be married to the minister of the facility.

If your search for an officiant must continue you might be surprised to know you can find an officiant in the Yellow Pages of your local telephone directory. There are various headings under which you will find people available to perform the ceremony. Look under "Clergy" or under the various "Wedding" sections. Many of these ministers are very flexible in their scheduling and can accommodate your wedding date. At the same time, you will want to interview these individuals carefully.

You will also find officiants who advertise in local wedding publications. Many of these publications are free and can be found where you register for wedding gifts. These publications are chock full of wedding vendors who can assist you in every aspect of your planning. Other ministers may advertise in the local edition of a national wedding magazine. These magazines may be ordered online or obtained at your local bookstore or grocery store.

More and more you are able to find ministers on the Internet with their own webpage. I have had a website since 1996 (www.wedding-ceremony.com) and couples seem to greatly enjoy the information about me, my wedding ideas, and the services I offer. Many times when I meet a couple for the first time both people already know about me, what I look like, and how I can be of assistance to them. The Internet contains a wealth of wedding information. The more you know the better decisions you can make. The amount of information you can obtain and the comparison shopping you can do is greatly enhanced online. But you must be a careful and informed consumer.

In my opinion, you should always meet the person long before the wedding. Make sure you like the person. Your officiant will also most likely appear in some of your wedding pictures. You want those pictures to bring back fond memories of people who were part of your big day. The better you know your wedding minister the more likely you will have grown to like the person who joined you in marriage. In my opinion, the officiant should desire that your wedding dreams come true almost as much as you do.

What Should We Talk About?

Unfortunately, it is often difficult beginning a conversation with a minister. There are certain ideas, notions, and attitudes that are often associated with clergy. We may think to ourselves, "What if the minister knew I have not been in church for several years," or "What if the minister knew we have been living together for many months?" What we forget is that ministers are just people too. They have the same doubts and fears as anyone else.

Talk to your prospective officiant as you would with anyone else. Talk to the minister about how the two of you met, talk to the minister about your wedding, talk to the minister about things that are important to both of you. You might be interested to know what is important to the minister. Why does he or she perform wedding ceremonies? How many weddings has this person performed? How many weddings does she perform on any given weekend? What are his credentials? Make sure he or she meets any state requirements.

A word of warning is appropriate here. All wedding officiants are not the same with regard to credentials. Make sure you know what you are getting by asking very specific questions.

What Should We Ask?

First of all, ask if the officiant will have any problems coming to your wedding site if it is not in a church. If your dream wedding takes place on a ranch amongst bales of hay, make sure the minister knows that. Frankly, most ministers you find through an advertisement will do just about anything you would like.

Also, find out if their ceremony is written in stone or if you can change, edit, or amend it to suit your tastes and beliefs. If the minister gives only one choice of ceremony make sure it reflects your belief system. If the ceremony does not reflect your belief system, and the officiant is unwilling to offer another type of ceremony, find someone else to assist you.

Ask if there are any special celebrations that might be incorporated into the ceremony. You may want something different from the traditional Unity Candle. Does the prospective officiant have any suggestions? You may have children from another marriage and want them included in the ceremony. Does the prospective officiant offer avenues through which you can accomplish this?

Ask if the minister will be giving a sermon during the ceremony. As we have seen, people can tell horror stories of their best friend being completely shocked when the minister gave a sermon in the middle of the ceremony. If you do not agree with the topic of the sermon it would be best to get this out in the open for discussion long before the ceremony takes place. Ask if there will be any surprises of this sort at your wedding.

It is also advisable to ask where the officiant attended seminary or divinity school. Ask to see diplomas or their ordination certificate. Make sure the institution granting the degree is accredited by the Association of Theological Schools. You may be asking, "Why is this so important?"

Well, unfortunately there are many wedding ministers who have been "ordained" by simply clicking a button on the Internet. This is perfectly legal in most states because the state does not and cannot interfere with religious issues. The state will not, and cannot by mandate of the United States Constitution, tell a religious institution how to regulate or educate their clergy.

You merely have to type in "become ordained" in any Internet search engine and with a couple of clicks you too (or your best friend) can preside over wedding ceremonies. There has been several television comedies in which a friend is ordained through the mail or over the Internet to perform the nuptials. Many times the humor is provided at the expense of the couple because the wedding turns into a fiasco. If it is important to you that your minister be ordained in a more conventional way, ask to see their credentials or diplomas.

Payment

Most often you will want to compensate the minister for attending and presiding over your ceremony. But what is a fair rate? After all, the ceremony was only 20–30 minutes long and we offered free food at the reception. The officiant does not really work that hard, right?

Wrong. Any minister who takes your wedding seriously will be under a great deal of pressure at the time of your event. The minister should want your ceremony to be special too. The number one fear in the United States is not death, as many people might suspect. The number one fear is public speaking. Most people say they would rather die than get up in front of hundreds of people and speak! Your minister must perform close to flawlessly for your wedding. That creates a great deal of pressure.

Some ministers will have a set fee they charge. Some regions of the country seem to have a higher rate of offering to wedding ministers than do others. Most authentic ministers will leave the amount of the offering up to the couple's discretion. In this case, you might want to ask the minister what the average couple offers in the way of compensation.

Keep in mind that many ministers are supported for the most part by a church or religious institution. Their sole source of income is usually not performing weddings so they typically are not charging very much in the way of fees. This would most often be the case if you are using your own church minister. Ministers of a church may ask you to make a donation to the church rather than a payment for his or her services. There are also many retired ministers who use weddings to supplement their income. Then there are other ministers who have left the church as a pastor but did not lose their ordination privileges.

For the minister attempting to earn a living solely through weddings he or she will be very busy. That minister must do many, many weddings if his or her entire income is derived from performing weddings. Think about the amount of money you offer the minister and multiply that number by 52. That number is the gross amount the minister will make in one year if she or he is scheduled to perform one wedding *every* weekend. Think about how you found the minister. Was it through advertising? Advertising costs must come off the gross amount. The gasoline for his or her vehicle, etc. must come off the gross amount. The wedding ministry "business" is not often very lucrative. One must perform multiple weddings every weekend in order to be profitable. Your officiant will hopefully be performing weddings as a labor of love not as a business venture.

In the event your minister has come as part of your wedding package at a hotel or resort, you usually need not pay the typical amount as the resort or hotel has often compensated the minister. You might still be gracious and offer the minister a tip if you have received excellent service. I suggest you just make sure you understand the financial situation and expectations so as to avoid any possible embarrassment for you or the minister.

Wedding ministry is a glorious and rewarding way of assisting couples. And while I am certainly biased, I believe the professional wedding minister is poorly compensated. The minister is usually paid the least of all the services provided at a wedding. It is not at all uncommon for the wedding cake to cost more than what couples offer the minister. And as stated previously, you can still get married if the cake gets ruined but not if the minister is not present.

How Do I Know If I Am Choosing The Right Officiant?

It is always difficult to know for sure that the officiant you choose will be the best available on your wedding day. Above all, make sure you are completely comfortable with the person and the answers you received from your questions. You may also want to ask for referrals from other couples the officiant has worked with recently.

Do not be pressured into making a decision at the time of your meeting if you do not feel comfortable in doing so. If a minister pressures you to decide at that very moment you may want to seek out someone else to officiate your wedding. The wedding minister should rarely be in the position of high-pressured sales.

The decision you make will last a lifetime of memories. Be sure the memories will be happy ones by choosing the right wedding officiant. And also make sure you, as the couple, are the focal point of the wedding. It is my opinion that the minister should facilitate your wedding, not be a showman or star. You two are the stars. The celebrant should make you look good. Not the other way around.

5

Premarital Counseling: Who Needs It!

o o o o o o o o o o o o o o o o o o o o o o o o o o o o o o o o o

"Love is a fire.
But whether it is going to warm your heart
or burn down your house,
you can never tell."

—Joan Crawford

Tami and Paul were going through my premarital counseling sessions. They had both previously been married and did not want to make the same mistakes that occurred in their first marriages. To Tami and Paul this meant premarital counseling. As we ended our final session both commented that this information would have been useful in previous relationships. They had been skeptical about premarital counseling in the past. They were believers now.

The simple answer to the question of "Who needs premarital counseling?" is EVERYONE. Some people, particularly the male gender of our species it seems, are afraid of counseling of any type. The sharing of feelings, the fear of exposure, and sometimes just having to talk at all are not areas of great comfort for many men.

So, it may be important to remember that premarital counseling does not intend to discover the "bad" in a relationship, but it attempts to provide the couple with tools by which both individuals can enhance and enrich their marriage. Premarital counseling is rarely used to test whether or not you two should be married. In fact, many of the tools in premarital counseling are merely meant to increase couple communication, expectations and to encourage goal setting.

How Do I Find A Counselor?

The first type of premarital counseling which is most familiar is that required by a minister, church, or denomination/religion. Many times this type of premarital counseling must be completed in an allotted time before the minister will marry you in the church/synagogue or will allow the sacrament of marriage to take place within its walls. Make sure of your minister's requirements and expectations before planning a wedding date. These classes or sessions may require anything from a few meetings to several months.

If you are getting married outside of the church you may want to find a pastoral counselor. There are pastoral counselors who specialize in premarital counseling. The American Association of Pastoral Counselors says that, "Pastoral Counseling is a unique form of psychotherapy which uses spiritual resources as well as psychological understanding for healing and growth. Pastoral Counselors are certified mental health professionals who have had in-depth religious and/or theological training." These individuals are usually affiliated with a particular denomination or organization and can often develop a program specifically to meet your needs. A diagnostic assessment may be used in order to get a better idea of the couple's priorities, needs, and desires. The couple usually retains a great deal of control throughout the process.

Pastoral counselors have usually gone through a great deal of education and training. Most often the pastoral counselor will have at least a master's degree in theology in addition to another master's or doctoral degree in counseling or psychology. If you are interested in finding a pastoral counselor you should contact the American Association of Pastoral Counselors at 703.385.6967 (http://www.aapc.org). Another good organization is The International Association of Pastoral Counselors (http://www.iapcinc.org).

Another counseling option is that of a Licensed Professional Counselor or Licensed Marriage and Family Therapist. The couple, again, retains a great deal of control with these providers. They will also often use a diagnostic multiple choice type assessment to ascertain the couple's needs. These counselors will often have times for sessions that are convenient to your schedule. Most often these counselors have a minimum of a master's degree in academic preparation. They are usually licensed by the state or a national organization such as the National Board of Certified Counselors (http://www.nbcc.org), the American Counseling Association (http://www.counseling.org), and the American Association of Marriage and Family Therapists (http://www.aamft.org). These counselors can easily be found in the Yellow Pages under the section "marriage counselors." You might check to see if your insurance or employment has a mental health benefit that might be used for premarital counseling. Probably the best way to find a counselor is to obtain a recommendation from a friend or family member who has had a good experience with that particular counselor.

Another great resource is the membership of the Coalition of Marriage, Family and Couples Education. The coalition provides training and support for organizations and individual marriage educators. A directory of programs is listed on their webpage (http://www.smartmarriages.com). This organization continues to grow and expand as new research indicates how important successful marriages are to our society.

Whatever you do, be sure to find a counselor that meets your needs and expectations. You will probably be spending about 12 hours in sessions with the counselor. Make sure you are comfortable with this person and his or her approach to premarital counseling.

What To Expect In Counseling

I am of the opinion that all couples will have areas of strength in their marriage. All couples will also have areas of improvement for their marriage. Many marriage educators use an instrument called PREPARE developed by David Olson at the University of Minnesota. This instrument is excellent in examining 13 areas that have proven to be significant in marital satisfaction. These areas are: 1) Communication; 2) Conflict Resolution; 3) Personality Issues; 4) Financial Management; 5) Marital Satisfaction; 6) Leisure Activities; 7) Children and Parenting; 8) Family and Friends; 9) Realistic Expectations; 10) Cohabitation Issues; 11) Idealistic Distortion; 12) Role Relationship; and 13) Spiritual Beliefs.

The power of the PREPARE instrument is not that it tells you whether or not to be married. You have already made the decision to wed. The power of the PREPARE assessment lies in diagnosing marital difficulties that may arise in the future. These difficulties can best be confronted by an educated and prepared couple. For instance, if the assessment reveals the two of you are dissimilar with regard to your beliefs of Family and Friends (No. 8 above) you can then use the skills taught by the minister or counselor in the premarital education sessions when issues arise.

Many counselors, ministers, and educators are now using the RELATE inventory. The inventory is available to you online (http://relate.byu.edu) and is very fun and inexpensive. If you do nothing else for your marriage please consider taking this assessment on the web.

After taking an assessment or questionnaire the majority of your counseling will be discerning the similarities and differences the two of you will likely confront in your marriage. Teaching you the skills necessary to handle these issues constructively will be the lessons you can take from your time with the counselor or minister.

Alternatives To Counseling

I do not believe there is anything better for your marriage than meeting with the minister or, better yet, a bona fide licensed counselor in sessions designed to assist you in your life together. Yet, there will be couples who, for a variety of reasons, do not believe premarital counseling is applicable to their situation. Many couples are so caught up in the initial stages of their relationship that they believe marital problems will never be a factor in their relationship. This way of thinking is naïve at best. Your relationship and your marriage *will* change with time and counseling will help you prepare for those changes.

If you cannot sit still for a few sessions with a counselor you might think about the possibility of attending a marriage seminar. While these seminars cannot give you individualized instruction that comes with premarital counseling, they can give you a great deal of information you will hopefully incorporate into your marriage.

For some couples, the seminar format is the least threatening of any of the options discussed above. You are together with several other couples in a weekend retreat or a one-day seminar. The amount of money associated with attending these seminars is often very reasonable. My favorite seminar is the Prevention and Relationship Enhancement Program (PREP). You can find out a great deal more about PREP from their webpage (http://www.prepinc.com).

This program is very well researched and has been shown to enhance couples relationship satisfaction. Very briefly, PREP course entitled "Fighting for Your Marriage" explains:

The Tremendous Joy of Connecting...

Marriage can be an oasis of acceptance and appreciation. For everyone who wants to be understood, here's a simple but effective tool to bring insight and closeness to your relationships.

Four Danger Signs...

Research has revealed the top reasons that marriages are weakened or even destroyed. Learn about the four key risk factors and the steps you can take to eliminate all these kinds of danger signs from your relationship.

Viva La Difference!

Gain fresh insights into why men and women see life so differently. You'll leave with a whole new appreciation for who you are—and whom you love.

Enjoy the Good Times...

More than "Don't worry, Be Happy", learn the secrets of keeping busyness from crowding out the fun in your marriage.

No Matter What!

All of us need to improve our skills when it comes to loving the most important people in our lives. It doesn't matter whether you have a newfound love, you're gritting your teeth as your teen gets his license, or your youngest has left you with an empty nest. The Fighting for Your Marriage workshop is your chance to learn the insights and skills to help you enjoy your marriage no matter where you are today or what tomorrow may bring.

If You Do Nothing Else

If you do not attend counseling sessions or attend a seminar at the very least have a very serious discussion about your upcoming marriage and your expectations of one another. In my opinion this is the least effective or desirable option for couples. With that being said, you must be able to discern the things you will not tolerate in your marriage. It is important that your mate be told these things rather than having to assume or guess your needs and/or desires.

All of us need to improve our skills when it comes to loving the most important people in our lives. At the very least the two of you should examine the following:

- Personal Attitudes

- Ambitions and Goals

- Religion

- Communication

- Friends and Recreation

- Finances

- Residence

- Health

- Sexual Relations

- Child rearing

- Relationships with Parents

- Relationships with In-laws

The expectations you have of one another may prove to be the undoing of your marriage if you do not take preventative measures. Make sure you both understand, and agree with, the expectations and needs of one another. If it is truly "death 'til you part" you will both want all (or at least most) of those days to be happy ones. Premarital counseling and education can be a very positive factor in your relationship success.

6

The Best Man,
Maid of Honor & Ushers

○ ○
"What the world really needs is
more love and less paperwork."

—Pearl Bailey

Russ and Laura were married in a beautiful ceremony. They had completed a great deal of the planning themselves and had done a wonderful job. Russ and Laura made sure that each of their attendants was informed of the traditional duties for their roles in the wedding and reception. Their attendants were very thankful for Russ and Laura's attention to this detail because they were able to help with the wedding at a much higher level. Only two of the attendants had ever been in a wedding before.

Unfortunately many couples do not do as Russ and Laura did. They often believe people will instinctively know what to do within their wedding role. For instance, if you hope or expect that someone will give a toast at your reception it is much better to let that person know in advance so they might have an opportunity to prepare a fitting toast.

The Best Man has a large number of duties to fulfill. Because of this I have devoted the majority of this chapter to the traditional duties of the Best Man. However, there is also information about your maid of honor and ushers. You have given a tremendous compliment when asking someone to serve as an attendant in your wedding. Yet at the same time you have bestowed an incredible responsibility. It is very important that you help your attendants know what they should be doing in order to fulfill their roles and responsibilities.

The Best Man

Having been involved in hundreds of weddings I can instantly spot an ill prepared Best Man. Some of the blame for a poorly prepared Best Man must be shared by the groom or the consultant if one has been used. The groom should help the Best Man realize the responsibilities that accompany the role. In fact, next to the bride, the Best Man has the most wedding tasks to be performed and can help a wedding and reception flow much more smoothly.

So that you are not left guessing what the Best Man should do, I have briefly outlined and explained the duties below. While the groom may not ask or desire for all of these duties to be completed, it is imperative the two of you have a conversation about the duties to be carried out. As the groom, you may want to give your Best Man a duty roster edited from my remarks below.

◆   ◆   ◆

The Best Man is:

- *The Clothing coordinator*—the Best Man should make sure all rented clothing has been ordered. Most likely the Best Man will be responsible for picking up and returning the clothing to the shop for all of the male wedding party members. Make sure too that all accessories (i.e., ties, gloves, ascots, cufflinks, etc.) are received and how to use them so you can assist others.

- *The Usher Coordinator*—make sure you understand the duties and responsibilities of the ushers. You should be able to help them remember who to seat where and when (see more below).

- *The Bachelor Party Coordinator*—traditionally the Best Man has coordinated this event. Dating back to Roman times, the party has been seen as the final fling of a man before he is "tied down" to one woman. Be cautious here. While the event should be memorable, you do not want the bride to despise you for the rest of your life because of a bachelor party. If you envision a raucous evening of drinking, plan the event a week in advance of the ceremony. You do not want the groom to be physically ill on his wedding day. Take necessary precautions like renting a limousine or having a designated driver. Thankfully the trend is moving away from these types of parties and towards entire affairs built around sporting themes such as golf. Use your imagination and be safe!

- *The Gift Giver*—collect money from the ushers and groomsmen to buy a gift from you all. Make sure to allow time for engraving or monogramming if necessitated by the gift. Usually you can make the presentation with all the men at hand prior to the ceremony. Think of what you will say in advance. Make the occasion memorable for your relationship with the groom is soon likely to change. Additionally, you will be a great hit if you personally have roses or champagne delivered to the couple's hotel room or cruise line cabin!

- *Personal Assistant*—you are basically the valet or servant of the groom. You will help him in arranging the honeymoon, packing for the trip, making sure he has the wedding license and a passport if necessary, getting the luggage to the airport and checking it in, giving him the claim checks, etc. Whew!

- *Time Keeper*—you should make sure the groom is always on time. Assist him in getting dressed, to the ceremony location, leaving the reception (with the bride), and to the dock or airport with time to spare.

- *Money Keeper*—it is usually the responsibility of the Best Man to see that the officiant is paid. However, the fee is most often given to the Best Man by the groom. Make sure you are aware of the arrangement in advance of the wedding ceremony. Wedding officiants often do not want to embarrass anyone by having to ask for their fee.

- *Transportation Guru*—you may need to drive the groom to the ceremony location. You may be asked to drive the couple from the ceremony to the reception if chauffeured limousines are not used. Airport runs are also not uncommon. If they are using their own "get-away car" the Best Man will often see that the vehicle is appropriately decorated. Use precautions so that paint is not damaged or that embarrassing sayings or phrases are not used.

- *Speechmaker*—you will toast the new couple at the reception. This responsibility takes time and preparation and for many, is a gut wrenching experience (you may refer to the toasting tips in this book). Remember this: You do not have to be an accomplished orator to make a successful wedding toast.

- *Master of ceremonies*—be prepared to introduce the wedding party at the reception and to announce the dances that traditionally accompany the reception. Most often these duties are left to the band leader or disc jockey. Find out about this task in advance.

- *Dancer*—you will usually have the fourth dance with the bride. She will dance with the groom, her father, her father-in-law, and then you. If you are blessed with two left feet you may want to find out what kind of dance is expected and take a lesson or two.

As you can see, there is a great deal more to being a Best Man than just holding the bride's ring during the ceremony. The Best Man is essentially the assistant or valet of the groom for a period of time. The Best Man should take a few moments to map out and organize his responsibilities. One cannot be overly prepared to be a Best Man.

The most important piece of advice I can offer the Best Man is summed up in one word: ASK!! The Best Man should take the time to sit down with the bride and groom and ask them what they are expecting. By asking questions the Best Man leaves nothing to risk and will surely have a couple who appreciates his efforts and sincerity.

◆　　　◆　　　◆

As the couple reading this book, you can also help your Best Man by making your expectations known without him having to ask. Do not be embarrassed to ask for what you want. Let him know of the duties that have been outlined here but also allow him the flexibility to make additions or deletions.

It is hoped the Best Man will take great pride and revel in the fact that he has been chosen to perform these duties. The responsibilities should be taken seriously. You might suggest he prepare checklists, leave voice mail or e-mail reminders for specific tasks. As the wedding nears ask again if there is anything further that requires explanation. If the Best Man performs his services well the wedding will run smoother, the bride and groom will be less anxious, and you will have had the *best* Best Man.

The Maid of Honor

While the Best Man has more tasks to perform, the maid or matron of honor traditionally receives more attention. While you probably know this, it bears repeating that a maid of honor is an honor attendant who has not married. A matron of honor is a married woman chose by the bride to serve as her honor attendant.

Like the Best Man responsibilities, I have outlined the typical Maid of Honor roles below. Again, you may want to add or subtract from this list. Just make sure the Maid of Honor understands your expectations.

◆　　　◆　　　◆

The Maid of Honor is:

- **The Dressing Attendant**—traditionally you are asked to assist the bride as she dresses for the big event. WARNING: This is sometimes a very stressful time for the bride. Be understanding and gentle with the bride during this time.

- **Dress Caretaker**—there will be times during the ceremony when you should make sure the bride's dress looks its best. You may want to "fluff" the dress after the bride takes her place for the ceremony, returns from lighting the Unity Candle, or during the taking of pictures.

- **The Bouquet Holder**—at some point during the ceremony the bride will hand her bouquet to you. You will probably learn the time this is to occur during the rehearsal. However, be ready for the bouquet to come your way at any time in order to provide the bride with more flexibility.

- **Holder of the Ring**—you will, most likely, be holding the groom's ring until such time as the couple exchanges wedding bands. Again, the rehearsal should make this duty perfectly clear. Just be alert and you will have no problems with this responsibility.

- **The Dressing Attendant: Part II**—usually the maid or matron of honor assists the bride when she changes clothes to leave for the honeymoon. This is a great time to say goodbye to your formerly single friend.

As the maid or matron of honor you have been given a wonderful privilege to assist the bride. Congratulations and attend her well!

◆   ◆   ◆

The Ushers

Ushers have a great deal of responsibility but they often seem to be overlooked when folks are giving out directions. Like the duties of the Best Man and Maid of Honor I have listed below the duties for which ushers are generally used. Add or subtract duties as you see fit.

◆   ◆   ◆

The Ushers Should:

Boutonniere—pin the flower of your left lapel. It is often easier to have someone do this for you.

In Advance Part I—find out if you are responsible for escorting in all guests or just the grandparents and parents. Hint: Ask the bride. She will most often be glad to make sure you know her preference.

Know Your Right from Your Left—if you are escorting all guests, tradition asks that you seat guests of the bride on the left and groom on the right. It may help to imagine where the bride and groom stand during the ceremony.

Their guests will sit on that same side. This tradition is being used less and less so make sure you know what the bride wants to do.

In Advance Part II—make sure you know specifically the grandparent and/or parent you will be escorting. Most likely, you will escort these same dignitaries both up and back down the aisle.

Know the Order—ushers should memorize this order:Before the ceremony:First—Groom's Grandparents
Second—Bride's Grandparents
Third—Groom's Parents (Mother may light Unity Candle taper)
Forth—Bride's Mother (may light Unity Candle taper)After the ceremony (reverse order):First—Bride's parents
Second—Groom's Parents
Third—Bride's Grandparents
Fourth—Groom's GrandparentsCongratulations on a job well done!

◆   ◆   ◆

At the end of this book I have put the duties of the Best Man, Maid of Honor and Ushers into an appendix. You may want to copy these as I have presented the duties or reproduce them in a different format and in your own words. Whatever you do, you can help your attendants by giving them information and preparing them for your special day.

7

Wedding Toasts

○ ○

There is no difficulty that enough love will not conquer;
no disease that enough love will not heal;
no door that enough love will not open;
no gulf that enough love will not bridge;
no wall that enough love will not throw down;
no sin that enough love will not redeem…
It makes no difference how deeply seated may be the trouble;
how hopeless the outlook; how muddled the tangle; how great
the mistake.
A sufficient realization of love will dissolve it all.
If only you could love enough you would be
the happiest and most powerful being in the world…

—Emmet Fox

Gina's father rose to give a toast to his little girl and new son-in-law. His words were thought provoking, inspiring, and brought tears to his eyes and to all who listened. Gina's father did not speak these words off the cuff. He had prepared in advance what he wanted to say, wrote it down, and did a great deal of work to memorize the toast.

A wedding toast can be a very touching part of your special day. It can also be somewhat painful when someone is not prepared and struggles for the words in front of all attending the event. As the newly married bride and groom, you might give a toast of thanks at the conclusion of the other speeches given that day. I thought it would prove beneficial for you to have some toasting tips that you might be able to give to others as well as for yourself. This short chapter is written for the benefit of all those who may be toasting at your wedding.

Cat Got Your Tongue?

The pressure! Toasters have a role in one of the greatest events of the season-your wedding! Many individuals have the "right" or, by tradition are requested, to give a toast at a wedding. I have outlined below some things people might want to think about if giving a wedding toast. While maybe not an all-inclusive list, after reading this you or your guests should be well on your way to a successful toast.

Who Goes When?

The order of wedding toasts may seem rather complicated at first. However, like many other etiquette issues, it will not be the absolute death of the day if any of these folks take their turn out of order. Participants should also be allowed the "right" to refuse making a wedding toast. The only person really required to give a wedding toast is the Best Man. Most likely, the Master of Ceremonies or the Best Man will have an agenda or script that tells him or her who should toast at what time.

Be sure and wait until all guests have been served their toasting beverage of choice before the toasting festivities begin. Incidentally, the server should pour the bride's drink first, followed by the groom, then the maid/matron of honor, then all of the other wedding party members. Traditionally the Best Man is to receive his beverage last.

The typical and traditional order of appearance for wedding toasts is:

1. Best Man

2. Fathers (groom's then bride's)

3. Groom

4. Bride

5. Friends and Relatives

6. Maid/Matron of Honor

7. Mothers (groom's then bride's)

8. Anyone else wishing to toast

What Should The Toaster Do?

The first thing the toaster should do is remain calm. Some people may never have had the opportunity to speak in front of a group about something as meaningful as two people loving one another and vowing to spend the rest of their lives together. How's that for a calming effect? One thing to keep in mind is that this should probably be the shortest speaking engagement you'll ever have. A toast should last no longer than five minutes with two minutes being more the norm.

The most important thing one can do is to prepare and practice. Take the toast seriously. At the same time, incorporate a funny story if possible. Look back during the time you've known the couple or the bride/groom and relate a personal story to the rest of those in attendance. Don't be afraid to get sentimental—even if you're a macho man. You will probably not have many opportunities to express yourself like this and folks really enjoy the sentiment! After all, weddings are emotional events.

What Should The Toaster NOT Do?

The biggest mistake I see time and again is when people attempt to get their speaking nerves up through the consumption of alcohol. You know your limits better than I, but you probably should have no more than two pre-toast drinks (if any at all!). An inebriated toaster is embarrassing to everyone and you'll spend a great deal of time wishing you had done things differently afterwards.

You should also not incorporate stories that will embarrass someone or jokes that are vulgar. These types of stories, jokes, and comments only make people feel uncomfortable. Making people uncomfortable is surely not the intention of your toast. Watch out as well for "insider" jokes and stories. While code language may be fun in many circumstances, you'll want everyone in the room to enjoy your speech.

In Brief

DO...	DON'T...
Be sure ahead of time that you are to give a toast	Joke at the expense of others.
Make a speaking agenda	Tell inappropriate stories or use vulgar language
Use humor	Be afraid to show emotion
Prepare, prepare, prepare	Get toast-ed (don't drink too much)
Be sentimental	Use verbose language
Smile	Chew gum or talk too fast
Keep it short (Five minutes max.)	Sweat the small stuff

If Worse Comes To Worse…

In emergencies toasters might just want to memorize one of these short, yet poignant, toasts:

"May 'better and for worse" be far better than worse!"
"A toast to love and laughter and happiness ever after!"
"May all your tomorrows be promises come true!"
"I wish you joy of heart, peace of mind, and the beautiful blessing of love."
"May all your hopes and dreams come true, and may the memory of this day become more dear with each passing year."

With a little hard work and determination, your toast can be a memorable addition to any couple's wedding day. Make the most of your toasting time and help the bride and groom realize how much you care about them.

8

The Main Event: Your Wedding Ceremony

o o o o o o o o o o o o o o o o o o o o o o o o o o o o o o o o o
What lies behind us, and what lies before us are tiny
matters compared to what lies within us.

—Ralph Waldo Emerson

Kyra and Bill had a wonderful wedding ceremony. The words they spoke to one another were heartfelt and warm. The minister was austere yet not too formal. The music was a blend of inspirational and well-known popular songs. The ceremony left no doubt to those in attendance who these two were as a couple and who they hoped to become as a family. The wedding was simply marvelous.

As a minister, I feel the ceremony should be the focal point of the day. Many times it appears the reception has become the focal point of a wedding. Couples often want to get the ceremony over with as quickly as possible so they can get to the reception and the party. Like Kyra and Bill, you have the opportunity to tell people what matters most to you through the wedding ceremony. It does take work to find the right words. I believe the results are well worth the effort.

Where to Get Married

For many couples this is a non-issue. Of course you will be married in a church, temple, mosque or other relevant religious structure. Maybe this is the place where you met, perhaps this is the place where one of you grew up, possibly this is your new religious home for your married life.

For other couples the decision is not so easy. Not belonging to a religious organization these couples must look for another wedding venue. I encourage you to use your imagination when looking for a place to wed.

There are probably plenty of wedding chapels in larger towns and cities from which to choose. Look also at private colleges and universities in your area. Often these institutions will have splendid facilities.

You might also look at city gardens to have a beautiful outdoor wedding. Perhaps a museum is more your style or a country club. A local winery can provide a very festive location for a wedding (see Chapter Nine for wine cup ceremony). Have you thought of getting married on a big boat or on top of a mountain? Think of fun places where you have gone on dates or hold dear to your heart. Give yourself permission to think about having fun with your choices. Couples who laugh and have fun are often well on their way to relationship success.

Outdoor Weddings

In thinking about where to get married you must decide if the venue will be outdoors or inside. If you are getting married in a garden or park you will have no choice but to contend with the weather that day. That may be no problem at all where you live. In most of the United States the weather may have some bearing on your choices.

Outdoor weddings can be extraordinarily beautiful and are often the most appropriate choice for your ceremony. However, they can also be extraordinarily painful under certain circumstances. In Texas, where I live, outdoor weddings in the summer wearing a traditional wedding dress and tuxedos can be quite uncomfortable.

You should also consider your guests if having an outdoor wedding. The comfort of your guests will have a direct correlation on their enjoyment of your big day. There have been many times when guests have come up to me after a ceremony and said something to the effect of, "What were those two thinking when they decided to have the wedding and reception outside!"

Here, then, are a few tips for an outdoor wedding that you may want to consider:

- **Clothing**—you might consider clothing that is different than traditional tuxedo and gown. More casual dress and even festive Hawaiian garb may be more appropriate. Encourage your guests to dress accordingly so they will be more comfortable as well.

- **Unity Candle**—you might consider eliminating the Unity Candle from an outdoor ceremony. Any slight breeze will blow out your candle and make lighting the center candle more difficult.

- **Reception**—you might consider having your reception indoors. If the weather during the ceremony was unpleasant you do not want to prolong that feeling for you or your guests.

- **Ceremony length**—you might consider having a rather short ceremony if it is possible the weather will turn bad. Your guests will often be appreciative.

- **Water**—you might consider have plenty of water and paper fans available for your guests.

- **Have a backup**—you might want to consider having a backup plan to your outdoor wedding. If it rains where will you go? If it is 112 degrees do you really want elderly family members and friends outside?

Ceremony Structure

Most ceremonies will follow the same basic structure. You will see this structure in the ceremonies that follow in the next chapter. Most ceremonies will open with a welcome by the officiant to all who are attending. This will often, although not necessarily, be followed by the giving of the bride. The officiant will often follow this with inspirational words about marriage.

The vows of the couple follow. The vows are most often prepared words repeated after the officiant. Additionally the bride and groom may choose to recite personal vows to one another. The giving and receiving of rings often follow the vows. Many couples then light the unity candle or another ritual. A kiss and benediction or departing words will often close the service.

It may look something like this:

Processional

This is, of course, the portion of the ceremony where the bridal party makes their way up the aisle to be greeted by the groom and his band of attendants. This is usually accompanied by music. In the processional you might want to examine the way people proceed up the aisle. You may want to take a look at what it historically means for the father to "give away" his daughter. You may want to play the music of you favorite contemporary musical artist rather than J.S. Bach. The officiant will likely make some introductory remarks.

Declaration of Consent

This is the part of the ceremony that is required to make the union legal in most states. It is the "I Dos." This is where each party says they are coming into the marriage of their own free will. It usually takes the form of something like, "Do you Gayle, take Russell, to be your lawful husband in good times and in bad, etc." Gayle would respond with an "I Do" stating for all to hear that she desires to be married to this man. So, while you do have to take and receive the other in marriage, you can say this in a variety of ways. Be creative!

Readings

In our culture the reading we most often associate with weddings are biblical. The writings of Paul, especially the "Love Chapter" in First Corinthians, are often used. However, you may find readings by poets, lyrics to special songs, or the words of a play to be more appropriate for your wedding. This might be a good place to get a friend involved by having one or two of them come up to deliver the readings.

Personal Vows of Bride and Groom

This is where you can tell your loved one how you feel about him or her. Many couples do not want to spend the time needed to adequately develop their personal vows. I suggest you talk about how you two met, how your love developed, and how you will nourish one another in the future and forever. There are many good books that will assist you in writing your vows.

Presentation of the Rings

The presentation of the rings is often scripted with tradition. I suggest that you look into different ways this has been done and choose the one that has the most meaning to the two of you.

The Ceremony of the Candles

Most ceremonies will include the Unity Candle. This is a time honored and beautiful tradition depicting how your two lives will now become one. At the same time, there are other ceremonies you might consider. Couples have shared a homemade loaf of bread amongst the bride and groom and then sent it out to the crowd to each have a small piece, others have shared a glass of wine or juice with the same unity idea as the candle, still others create their own ritual for their wedding that others are certain to imitate. This is often accompanied by music.

Recessional

This is very similar to the processional, of course. Make sure the music reflects the mood and temperament of your wedding. If you came in with classical you can still go out with rock and roll!

A Word About Personal Vows

In several of the ceremony examples that are found in the next chapter you will find the opportunity for couples to give personal vows. Personal vows are created by the couple and are recited to each partner. It is a way to express your personal feelings to your partner rather than simply repeating the words of the officiant.

Many of the couples I work with are reticent to create personal vows for their ceremony. Sometimes creating personal vows can just seem like one more thing to do for your wedding day. But consider carefully the possibility of not allowing your wedding day to pass without telling your partner how important he or she is to you. You will only have one wedding day. You can make this day even more special by sharing personal vows.

Couples will sometimes not know where to start when it comes to writing their personal vows. You might be surprised with how easy it can be to write these vows. I encourage couples to think about their first date, possibly their first kiss, or maybe the time when they knew beyond doubt they had found the right person with whom to spend the rest of their life.

Also, you do not have to rely on memory for your personal vows. I encourage couples to write their vows on note cards. Men may put their cards in a pocket or give to their Best Man. Woman can ask an attendant to hold her card. I suggest couples save these cards and bring them out for special occasions, such as anniversaries.

I hope you will choose to create personal vows for your wedding. In this instance you have this one wonderful opportunity to offer up your loving thoughts to everyone attending your wedding. Personal wedding vows will be talked about more than anything the officiant might say. People expect the minister to say things that are worthy of a wedding. Everyone listens when the couple utilizes personal vows to proclaim their love. There have been many occasions when I have had to wipe tears from my eyes because the couple had done so tremendously well with personal vows. I have yet to have one couple who was disappointed in taking the time and effort to create personal vows.

Ceremonies Without God

More and more couples come to me requesting that there be no mention of God in their ceremony. They want to have the pomp and circumstance associated with a wedding but do not believe (rightly or wrongly), a Justice of the Peace will provide what they desire. This no longer surprises me. The majority of my wedding ministry assists couples who do not have a church home but desire a reverent wedding ceremony. There are many personal reasons why people do not believe in God and, therefore, find no need to attend church services.

So, what are the options for couples who do not believe in God when it comes to their wedding ceremony? As best I can tell, there are indeed four options for these couples.

- Find a "regular" minister who will perform the ceremony of your choice or making

- Contact the Humanist Society

- Locate a local Unitarian Universalist minister

- Locate an Ethical Culture Society

One option is to find a minister who is open to adjusting his/her standard ceremony to reflect your beliefs, or rather, non-beliefs. I would suggest, however, that you request to see the ceremony in advance of the service so as not to be surprised by any uncomfortable wording or verbiage.

A better option might be to write your own ceremony and then find an officiant who is willing to deliver your creation. I think writing your own ceremony can be extremely rewarding for couples. Of course, it takes time and effort to create a wedding ceremony. But you would be assured by doing so that your beliefs or non-beliefs are readily apparent for all in attendance. Many ministers will be willing to work with you in this capacity.

A second, and possibly the best, option is to contact the Humanist Society. The Humanist Society ordains ministers who specialize in weddings, memorials, baby naming ceremonies (an alternative to baptism), and other rites of passage for individuals and couples who do not believe in God. These ceremonies are reverent, well thought out, and most likely will not be offensive to people attending your wedding. You can learn more about the Humanist Society through their webpage (http://www.humanist-society.org) or by calling (800) 837–3792.

A third option for a Godless ceremony is to contact a local Unitarian Universalist minister. These men and women come from a religious tradition that is liberal and inviting for all. In fact, in a UU fellowship you are just as likely to be sitting next to a Buddhist, an earth-centered spiritualist, or an agnostic as well as Christian. With all of this congregational diversity, UU ministers have become adept at providing the right ceremony for the needs of their members.

You can easily look up a UU minister on the web or under the "Churches" section of the Yellow Pages. There will be several UU churches or fellowships in larger metropolitan areas. A Unitarian Universalist minister's fee may be a bit higher than most local ministers. If my understanding is correct, their fee is set by the denomination and not by the minister. You may also find UUs through their association's website (http://www.uua.org)

Finally, you may be in an area that supports an Ethical Culture Society. You can find out if a Society is near you by visiting the American Ethical Union online (http://www.aeu.org). Ethical Culture focuses on "Deeds not creeds." The question of whether or not God exists is not as important as what you do in life that makes a difference on this earth in the here and now. Ethical Culture Societies are found mainly in the northeast United States although the movement is attempting to expand. Their website has a special link for those interested in weddings without God.

Now you have at least four options for a wonderful wedding ceremony for couples who do not believe in God. You will probably have more work to do in finding the right person for your ceremony. Make sure your officiant is in sympathy with your philosophy at the very least. You will not want his or her personal beliefs or feelings coming through and compromising your special day.

9

Ceremony Examples

o o o o o o o o o o o o o o o o o o o o o o o o o o o o o o o o o
Love is something eternal…
The aspect may change,
But not the essence

—*Vincent Van Gogh*

On the following pages I have included several ceremonies for you to peruse in order to assist you in creating a ceremony that is meaningful to you. I encourage couples to look at these ceremonies and others to find the words that best express their feelings. You might find something in one ceremony that you like and something else from another. If you desire, you can send me an e-mail through my webpage (http://www.marriage-education.net) and I will send you these ceremonies as an MS Word file so that you might cut and paste your ceremony together.

Ceremony number one was taken from a wonderful book compiled by Marty Younkin. Marty has graciously allowed me to share his ceremony here with you. His book, *A Wedding Ceremony to Remember*, is an excellent resource for wedding ceremonies. You may find more information about this book in Recommended Readings.

The remainder of the ceremonies presented here was given to me a number of years ago by a fellow minister. I have personally used all of these ceremonies. However, I have not been successful is uncovering the authorship of the ceremonies. If, during your own ceremony research, you are made aware of who wrote any of these ceremonies I would very much like to give them credit in upcoming editions of this book.

CEREMONY EXAMPLE
NUMBER ONE

Welcome

We would like to welcome all of you here today as we have come together in the presence of God to join (Bride) and (Groom) in holy matrimony. Marriage is a gift...a gift from God given to us so that we might experience the joys of unconditional love with a life-long partner. God designed marriage to be an intimate relationship between two people...mentally, emotionally, physically, and spiritually. This intimate relationship also gives us a picture of how much God wants to love and care for each one of us. Listen to the vows God made to you and to me that are recorded for us in the Word: *"I will betroth you to myself forever in lawful wedlock and unfailing devotion and love; I will commit myself to you, to have and to hold, and you shall know the Lord."* Because your deep love for each other comes from God above, this is a sacred moment, and it is with great reverence that I now ask you...

Consent

(Groom), do you take (Bride) to be your wedded wife, to live together after God's ordinance in the holy estate of matrimony? Do you promise to love her, comfort her, honor and keep her in sickness and in health, and forsaking all others, remain faithful to her as long as you both shall live? Groom's response: "I Do!"

And (Bride), do you take (Groom) to be your wedded husband, to live together after God's ordinance in the holy estate of matrimony? Do you promise to love him, comfort him, honor and keep him in sickness and in health, and forsaking all others, remain faithful to him as long as you both shall live? Bride's response: "I Do!"

Who gives (Bride) to be married to (Groom)? Escort's response: Her mother and I do!

Address

Please be seated…Today is the beginning of a new life together for you, Groom and for you Bride. It marks the commencement of new relationships to your families, your friends, and to each other. God knew your needs when you were brought together. God knew exactly what you needed to make you complete; and now, God wants you to commit yourselves to accept each other as the one who completes you. There are five little pearls of wisdom I want to share with you as you begin this new journey together.

First, LISTEN. Listen to each other; try to hear what your partner is really saying. The scripture says: *"Be quick to hear, slow to speak, and slow to anger."* What you say and how you say it is the foundation upon which to build your marriage. Take the words you hear from each other into your heart and let them become building blocks for a solid marriage…stepping stones to happiness. Say things that will encourage and build each other up. Communication is so important in a marriage, and so, take the time to talk with each other, but more importantly, take time to LISTEN.

Second, LEARN. Learn from each other. Both of you are different in so many ways. You bring certain abilities and specific traits into the relationship; but don't become threatened by the other person's strengths, gifts, or talents. Join forces so to speak; receive the other person's strengths and build upon them because you both have so much to give this marriage. The Bible says, *"Husbands, live with your wives in an understanding way."* So, Groom, your life-long assignment is to try to understand this woman. What makes her tick? What makes her happy? What makes her sad? What makes her secure? What makes her respond? What an assignment! If you learn from each other, you will be a better person for it, and your marriage will grow stronger because of it. So LEARN all you can about each other.

Listen, learn and third, LABOR…or work. Be willing to work on your relationship. Someone said, *"Anything worth having in this life is worth working for."* It's worth the effort. Work on your relationship. Make every effort to make this the very best marriage on God's earth. You don't find precious gems just lying around on top of the ground. You have to dig and work hard to get to them. But once you find them, it is worth every bit of effort that was made. So too, if you work at your relationship, it will be like finding those precious gems, and you'll strike it rich because of all your LABOR.

Listen, Learn, Labor, and fourth, LAUGH. Learn to laugh. Learn to laugh at yourself and learn to laugh at each other. The Bible says that *"laughter is good medicine."* Getting married is a serious step, and it should be taken seriously; but I am serious when I say that having fun and being able to laugh at our mistakes and our shortcomings goes a long way in solidifying the mortar of this institution we call marriage. Studies have shown that laughter has a profound and positive effect on the body. Laughter is the best medicine for a long and happy life. He who laughs…lasts. So the best way to make your marriage work is to play.

Listen, Learn, Labor, Laugh and finally, LOVE. What is love? And who am I to talk to you about that today? I can see it in your eyes. Countless songs have been written about it. Poems too many to number have been penned describing it. Books as numerous as the stars in the sky have been authored by both men and women to tell us all about it. But the one book that rises above them all, the Bible, says this about love: *"Love is very patient and kind, never jealous or envious, never boastful or proud, never haughty or selfish or rude. Love does not demand its own way nor is it irritable or touchy. It does not hold grudges and will hardly ever notice when others do it wrong. It is never glad about injustice, but rejoices whenever truth wins out. This kind of love knows no boundaries to its tolerance, no end to its trust, no fading of its hope, no limit to its endurance. It can outlast anything. Love is, in fact, the one thing that still stands when all else has failed."* So you can see, love is not just something you feel, it is something you do. Groom, it has been said, *"If you treat your wife like a queen, she will treat you like a king."*

And so…*LISTEN, LEARN, LABOR, LAUGH, and LOVE.* Practice these five things and your marriage will grow into a lifelong partnership that will endure the challenges of life and stand the tests of time.

Vows

Now Groom, please repeat after me. I Groom take thee, Bride,/to be my wedded wife/to have and to hold/from this day forward/for better, for worse/for richer, for poorer,/in sickness and in health,/to love and to cherish,/till death do us part./ This is my solemn vow.

And now Bride, please repeat after me. I Bride take thee, Groom,/to be my wedded husband/to have and to hold/from this day forward/for better, for worse/for richer, for poorer,/in sickness and in health,/to love and to cherish,/till death do us part./This is my solemn vow.

Explanation of The Rings

The wedding ring serves as a symbol of the promise you have just spoken. It is the outward and visible sign of an inward and invisible love which binds your hearts together. The wedding ring is also a symbol of what God is. God is without beginning and without end. God is eternal; and as you can see, your rings are without beginning and without end. So I believe that this exchange of rings not only reminds us of the unending love you have for each other, but also reflects the eternal love God has for each of you.

Ring Exchange Vows

May we have the token of Groom's love for Bride? Groom, please repeat after me. With this ring I thee wed/and from this day forward/I give thee my pledge/with tenderness and care/and trust in God.

And now may we have the token of Bride's love for Groom? Bride, please repeat after me. With this ring I thee wed/and from this day forward/I give thee my pledge/with tenderness and care/and trust in God.

Lighting of The Unity Candle

The lighting of the unity candle is a symbol of the union created by a man and a woman who enter into marriage. They are no longer two but one. The Bible says, *"For this cause a man shall leave his father and mother, and shall cleave to his wife, and the two shall become one flesh."* Today we see two people who have come to unite themselves as one…as one in the flesh and as one in the spirit. These candles symbolize that union. The outer candles represent the individual lives of Groom and Bride and the families from which they came; so the lighting of the unity candle not only symbolizes the coming together of these two individuals, but also the joining together of their families. May you all recognize your continuing importance in each other's lives by sharing with each other the light of your love.

Let us Pray

These two lives are now joined together as one. Groom and Bride, may these two rings symbolize the spirit of undying love in each of your hearts. Wherever you go, may you always return to one another in your togetherness. May you find in each other the kind of love for which everyone hopes; and may the home you establish be such a place of peace and joy that many will find there a friend. Amen.

Pronouncement

Groom and Bride, since you have consented together in holy matrimony and have pledged yourselves to each other by your solemn vows, by the giving of rings, and have declared your commitment of love before God and these witnesses, I now pronounce you husband and wife in the name of the Father and the Son and the Holy Spirit. Those whom God hath joined together, let no one separate.

Groom, you may now kiss your bride!

Ladies and gentlemen, it is my privilege to introduce to you for the first time Mr. and Mrs. Groom (however you would like to be introduced)!

CEREMONY EXAMPLE NUMBER TWO

Welcome

Friends and family of the Bride and Groom, what a joy it is to welcome you here, for we have come to celebrate the miracle of love and to witness the union of (Groom's Full Name) and (Bride's Full Name). Every experience you have ever had, every thing you have ever done, every thing you have ever learned has brought you to this moment as you now stand before these witnesses to take each other as husband and wife. New experiences lie before you with opportunities to grow deeper in love with each other. As you walk hand and hand into the future, cherish each moment as a gift—a gift given to strengthen the bond between you.

Consent

(Groom) and (Bride), as you give your hand to the other, are you both ready to be united as husband and wife? (Both answer): Yes.

Who presents (Bride) to be married to (Groom)?

(The Escort shall say one of the following): Her mother and I do; I do; We do; Her family does.

Address and Readings

Today, you are taking into your care and trust the happiness of the one person in the world whom you love with all your heart. You are agreeing to share life's deepest and richest experiences. You are adding to your life not only the affection of each other, but also the companionship and blessing of mutual respect. You have invited these guests to share in the celebration of your love, a love that now culminates in your union as husband and wife.

When you enter into marriage, you enter into life's most important relationship. It is a gift, given to bring comfort when there is sorrow, peace when there is unrest, laughter when there is happiness, and love when it is shared. Real love goes far beyond the feelings of romance and bliss. It is caring more about the well-being and happiness of your marriage partner than your own needs and desires. Love makes burdens lighter because you divide them. It makes joys more intense because you share them. It makes you stronger so you can become involved with life in ways you dare not risk alone. Real love says you are stronger together than when you are apart.

A successful marriage is not something that just happens. It takes work and it takes effort. Most importantly, it takes a commitment from both of you. A good marriage must be created. Listen to these words of wisdom on how to create a successful marriage.

The little things are the big things.
It is never being too old to hold hands.
It is remembering to say, "I love you" at least once a day.
It is never going to sleep angry.
It is at no time taking the other for granted; the courtship should not end with the honeymoon, it should continue through all the years.
It is having a mutual sense of values and common objectives; it is facing the world together.
It is forming a circle of love that gathers in the whole family.
It is doing things for each other, not in the attitude of duty or sacrifice, but in the spirit of joy.
It is speaking words of appreciation and demonstrating gratitude in thoughtful ways.
It is not expecting the husband to wear a halo or the wife to have the wings of an angel.
It is not looking for perfection in each other.
It is cultivating flexibility, patience, understanding, and a sense of humor.
It is having the capacity to forgive and forget.
It is giving each other an atmosphere in which each can grow.
It is finding room for the things of the spirit.
It is the common search for the good and the beautiful.
It is the establishing of a relationship in which the independence is equal, the dependence is mutual, and the obligation is reciprocal.
And finally, it is not only marrying the right partner, it is being the right partner.

Vows

(Groom), please repeat after me.

I, (Groom), take you (Bride),/to be my partner in life./I promise to walk by your side forever/and to love, help, and encourage you/in all that you do./I will take time to talk to you,/to listen to you,/and to care for you./I will share your laughter and your tears/as your partner, lover, and best friend./Everything I am and everything I have is yours/now and forevermore.

(Bride), please repeat after me.

I, (Bride), give myself to you (Groom),/on this our wedding day./I will cherish our friendship,/and love you today, tomorrow, and forever./I will trust you and honor you./I will love you faithfully/through the best and the worst,/through the difficult and the easy./What may come I will be there always./As I have given you my hand to hold,/so I give you my life to keep.

Rings

The wedding ring is the outward and visible sign of an inward and invisible bond which unites two loyal hearts in endless love. The ring is a circle which has no end and symbolizes the never-ending love that exists between you. The gold substance of which the ring is composed, is a symbol of the riches that reside in each of you. These rings are also made of precious gems, gems that radiate a quality and a brilliance that set them apart from other ordinary stones. May these rings always reflect the light of your love throughout your life together. Wear them as a sign of the love that exists between you, the love which now your hearts enfold and your words express.

May I have the token of (Groom's) love for (Bride)? (Groom), please repeat after me.

I give you this ring./Wear it with love and joy./As this ring has no end,/neither shall my love for you./I choose you to be my wife/this day and forevermore.

May I have the token of (Bride's) love for (Groom)? (Bride), please repeat after me.

This ring I give you/in token of my love and devotion/and with my heart/I pledge to you all that I am./With this ring I marry you/and join my life to yours.

Unity Candle

When the flames of two individual candles join together, a single brighter light is created by that union. May the brightness of this light shine throughout your lives, giving you courage and reassurance in the darkness. May its warmth give you shelter from the cold and may its energy fill your spirits with strength and joy. Now as you light this candle, may it symbolize that today you become as one…hand in hand, heart to heart, flesh to flesh, and soul to soul.

Blessing

Now you will feel no rain, for each of you will be shelter for the other. Now you will feel no cold, for each of you will be warmth to the other. Now there will be no loneliness, for each of you will be a companion to the other. Now you are two persons, but there is only one life before you. Go now to your dwelling place to enter the days of your togetherness. May beauty surround you both in the journey ahead and through all the years. May happiness be your companion and may your days together be good and long upon the earth. (Apache Blessing)

Pronouncement

(Groom) and (Bride), because you have committed yourselves to each other in marriage and demonstrated this by exchanging your vows and giving each other rings, I now pronounce you husband and wife.

Kiss

(Groom), you may kiss your Bride.

Presentation

Ladies and gentlemen, it is my privilege to introduce to you (Mr. and Mrs. However you would like to be introduced).

CEREMONY EXAMPLE
NUMBER THREE

Processional Music

If it were possible to begin this ceremony by gathering all the wishes of happiness for all present here…if we could gather together those precious wishes of affection and our very fondest hopes and turn them into music, we would be listening now to a most inspiring anthem, where it would be composed of the most harmonious notes possible to produce.

Even though this is not *quite* possible, just speaking of it should assure Bride and Groom that our hearts are attuned to theirs in these moments so meaningful to us all. For what greater thing is there for two human souls than to feel that they are joined together to strengthen each other in all labor, to minister to each other in all sorrow, and to share with each other in all gladness.

Who presents this woman in marriage?

(Response, "Her family and I do!" or other response of your choosing)

Please be seated. Marriage is an act of faith and a personal commitment as well as a moral and physical union between the couple. Marriage has been described as the best and most important relationship that can exist between two human beings; the construction of their love and trust into a single growing energy of spiritual life, it is a moral commitment that requires and deserves daily attention. Marriage should be a life-long consecration, backed with the will to make it last.

A reading from the Prophet says:
"True love gives nothing but itself
And takes nothing but from itself
Love does not possess, nor would it be possessed
For love is sufficient unto love.
Love has no other desire but to fulfill itself,
To awake at dawn with a winged heart and
Give thanks for another day of loving.
To rest at noon and meditate love's ecstasy;

To return home at eventide with gratitude,
And then to sleep with a prayer for the beloved in your heart
And a song of praise upon your lips."

(Kahlil Gibran, The Prophet)

Optional Old Testament or other Reading by friend (best man?) or officiant
Optional New Testament or other Reading by friend (maid of honor?) or officiant

Let us pray the Lord's Prayer together.
Our Father, who art in heaven, hallowed be thy name.
Thy kingdom come; Thy will be done; On earth as it is in heaven.
Give us this day, our daily bread.
And forgive us our trespasses; As we forgive those who trespass against us.
And lead us not into temptation; But deliver us from evil.
For thine is the kingdom and the power and the glory forever.
Amen.

Declaration of Consent

Groom do you take Bride to be your wedded wife, to love, to cherish, and to continually bestow upon her your heart's deepest devotion? (I DO)

And Bride, do you take Groom to be your wedded husband, to love, to cherish, and to continually bestow upon him your heart's deepest devotion? (I DO)

Please hold hands. Groom repeat after me:
Bride, you are consecrated to me now, as my wife, from this day forward, to love and to cherish, to have and to hold, for richer for poorer, for better and for worse, in sickness and in health, in sadness and in joy, to share together, as long as we both shall live." Amen.

And Bride, please repeat after me:
Groom, you are consecrated to me now, as my husband, from this day forward, to love and to cherish, to have and to hold, for richer for poorer, for better and for worse, in sickness and in health, in sadness and in joy, to share together, as long as we both shall live." Amen.

Optional Personal vows to Bride from Groom
Optional Personal vows to Groom from Bride

The Apostle Paul said about love:
"Love is patient; Love is kind; Love is not envious or boastful, or arrogant or rude. It does not insist on its own way; It is not irritable or resentful; It does not rejoice in wrongdoing. But rejoices in the truth. It bears all things, believes all things, hopes all things, endures all things."

Presentation of the Rings

What token of love do you offer your beloved?

(The rings are presented for blessing.)
Let us pray. Bless, O Lord these rings to be a sign of the vows by which this man and this woman have bound themselves to each other. May these rings be blessed as the symbol of this affectionate unity. These two lives are now joined in one unbroken circle. Wherever they go, may they always return to one another in their togetherness.

May these two find in each other the love for which all men and women yearn. May they grow in understanding and in compassion. May the home which they establish together be such a place of sanctuary that many will find there a friend. May these rings on their fingers symbolize the touch of the spirit of love in their hearts. Amen.

Groom, as you place the ring on Bride's finger repeat after me: "I give you this ring, as the pledge of my love, and as the symbol of our unity." Amen.

Bride, in placing the ring on Groom's finger repeat after me: "I give you this ring, as the pledge of my love, and as the symbol of our unity." Amen.

The Ceremony of the Candles

Our community is shared, if in a different way, by those who have passed beyond this life. Their roles in the lives of Bride and Groom are no less remembered and honored as we savor today's joyous moments. Join with us, then, in fond memory of all these people, and in particular we remember (Name/s of Deceased to be remembered). In their memory, let us be silent together.

In all the quiet of this very special moment, we pause, also, to be thankful for all the rich experiences of life that have brought Bride and Groom to this high point. We are grateful for the values which have flowed into them from those who have loved them and nurtured them and pointed them along life's way and for the values which they have found by their own strivings. We are grateful that within them is the dream of a great love and the resources to use that love in creating a home that shall endure.

As Bride and Groom light the candle, they do not extinguish their flames. Although they are embarking upon a new and unique relationship in the union of their lives in marriage, they, nonetheless, retain their own separate and unique identities and personalities.

(Bride and Groom will now light one candle from their two, symbolizing the union this marriage.)

Inasmuch as Groom and Bride have consented together in marriage before this company; Have pledged their faith and declared their unity by each giving and receiving a ring and are now joined in mutual esteem and devotion...by the power vested in me by the state of Texas as an ordained minister, I pronounce that they are husband and wife together and offer them this Benediction:

Let us pray. God, you have so consecrated the covenant of marriage that in it is represented the spiritual unity between Christ and His Church: Send therefore your blessing upon these your servants, that they may love, honor, and cherish each other in all faithfulness and patience, in wisdom and true Godliness, that their home may be a haven of blessing and peace; through Jesus our Lord, who lives and reigns with you and the Holy Spirit, one God, now and forever. Amen.

May God the Father, God the Son, God the Holy Spirit, bless, preserve, and keep you. May the Lord mercifully look upon you with favor and fill you with all the spiritual benediction and grace, that you may faithfully live together in this life, and in the age to come have life everlasting. Amen.

Groom you may kiss your bride.

Ladies and gentlemen, it is my privilege to introduce to you (Mr. and Mrs. However you would like to be introduced).

Recessional Music

CEREMONY EXAMPLE
NUMBER FOUR

Opening Words

We are gathered here, not to witness the beginning of what will be, but rather what already is! We do not create this marriage, because we cannot. We can and do, however, celebrate with Bride, Groom, and their families the wondrous and joyful occurrence that has already taken place in their lives.

So let the celebration begin!

The Processional

(Think of Musical Selection)

The Celebration Of Marriage

Marriage is a supreme sharing of experience and an adventure in the most intimate of human relationships. It is the joyous uniting of a man and a woman whose friendship and mutual understanding have flowered into romance. Today Bride and Groom proclaim their love to the world and we who are gathered here rejoice with them and for them in the new life they now undertake together.

Marriage is universally regarded as one of the crucial events of human life, taking its place with those other two—the coming hither in birth and the departure from life through death.

The joy we now feel is a solemn joy because the act of marriage is fraught with weighty consequences, both social and personal. By this marriage you two will reach a new social status and rise to a new plane of social dignity. But also, with the founding of the family, there will be the most difficult tasks and exacting disciplines which fall to our human lot.

Your marriage requires "love," which is a word often used with vagueness and sentimentality. We mean something very real, when we bind ourselves in love. When we love we see things other people do not see. We see beneath the surface and observe qualities which make this one different from and dearer than all others. To see with loving eyes is to know inner beauty and to be loved is to be seen and known as we are known to no other.

Such love means security. Each of us would like to have an absolute security. This we cannot have, but we come close to it when we are loved—when another human being wants us, wants to share life with us, accepts us, without qualification or reservation, not as perfect, but as human, with strengths and weaknesses.

The love of which we speak is not static. It is a growing and dynamic relationship. We dream that tomorrow we will grow and fulfill our possibilities. It is a blessing when someone believes in our dream of ourselves and wants to live with us and help make dreams and aspirations come true.

Love of this sort can grow. It is not, like youth, a moment that comes and is gone, remaining only a memory of something which cannot be recovered. It can grow because it has something to grow upon and grow with. It does not become contracted and stale, because it has for its object all the objects with which the two lovers are concerned. Love endures only when the lovers love many things together and not solely one another.

Optional Personal Vows by Groom
Optional Personal Vows by Bride

True love breeds unlimited courage and confidence. Such courage and confidence we know are yours as you continue your lives together under the ever embracing bond of marriage. In addition to the fund of affection and thoughtful consideration which you have for one another, you will need a capacity for self-sacrifice, patience and forbearance, for this is no light adventure which you are undertaking.

The secret of love and marriage is the emergence of the larger self. It is the finding of one's life by losing it. Such is the privilege of husband and wife—to be each himself, herself and yet another; to face the world strong, with the courage of two.

The high and fine art of married life is in this mutual enrichment, mental and spiritual, this give and take between two personalities, this mingling of two endowments which depletes neither, but enables each. The more he or she gives, to receive only the more.

Marriage is dedication. You give yourself, your life and love, into the hands of the one you love. You do so trustingly and generously. By the same token, each of you receives a gift—the life and love of the other. You receive this gift not only from the one you love, but also from the parents who brought you into the world and reared you and from the personal world of friends and family who are joined in friendship and faith in your marriage.

Bride and Groom believe that there should be equality between men and women in every relevant way and that it is especially important for this principle to be recognized in the marriage relationship. Marriage must be a cooperative venture in every sense. It is a relationship based on love, respect and a determination on the part of both wife and husband to adjust to each other's temperaments and moods—in health or sickness, joy or sadness, ease or hardship.

We are here to share your joy and hope and to speed you along the path which, henceforth, you are to tread together. May it be the path of blessedness, bright with the fragrant flowers of prosperity; a path of deepening and widening love that you shall travel arm in arm throughout eternity.

The Ceremony of the Candles

Our community is shared, if in a different way, by those who have passed beyond this life. Their roles in the lives of Bride and Groom are no less remembered and honored as we savor today's joyous moments. Join with us, then, in fond memory of all these people, and in particular we remember (Name/s of Deceased to be remembered). In their memory, let us be silent together.

In all the quiet of this very special moment, we pause, also, to be thankful for all the rich experiences of life that have brought Bride and Groom to this high point. We are grateful for the values which have flowed into them from those who have loved them and nurtured them and pointed them along life's way and for the values which they have found by their own strivings. We are grateful that within them is the dream of a great love and the resources to use that love in creating a home that shall endure.

As Bride and Groom light the candle, they do not extinguish their flames. Although they are embarking upon a new and unique relationship in the union of their lives in marriage, they, nonetheless, retain their own separate and unique identities and personalities.

(Bride and Groom will now light one candle from their two, symbolizing the union this marriage.)

The Commitment

This celebration is the outward token of an inward union of hearts, which we, together, bless and the state makes legal, but which neither state nor we together can create or annul. It is a union created by your loving purpose and kept by your abiding will. It is in this spirit and for this purpose that you have come here to be joined together.

Groom, will you have this woman to be your wedded wife, to live together in marriage; will you love her, comfort her, and honor her, in sickness and in health, in sorrow and in joy, so long as you both shall live?

Groom: I will!

Bride, will you have this man to be your wedded husband, to live together in marriage; will you love him, comfort him, and honor him, in sickness and in health, in sorrow and in joy, so long as you both shall live?

Bride: I will!

And will all you, here present, promise and commit yourselves to support and uphold this union of these two people? If so, please respond, "We will!"

Assembly responds: "We will!"

The Ceremony of the Rings

Traditionally, the marking of the passage to the status of husband and wife is marked by the exchange of rings. These rings are a symbol of the unbroken circle of love. Love freely given has no beginning and no end. Love freely given has no giver and no receiver—for each is the giver and each is the receiver. May these rings remind you always of the vows you have taken here today.

Groom: (Cued) This ring, a gift for you, symbolizes my desire that you be my wife from this day forward.

Bride: (Cued) This ring, a gift for you, symbolizes my desire that you be my husband from this day forward.

Inasmuch as Bride and Groom have consented together in this ceremony to live in wedlock and have witnessed their vows in the presence of this company, by the giving and receiving of rings, it gives me great pleasure to now announce that they are husband and wife!

And I ask that you treat yourselves and each other with respect, and remind yourselves often of what brought you together. Take responsibility for making the other one feel safe, and give the highest priority to the tenderness, gentleness and kindness that your connection deserves. When frustration, difficulty and fear assail your relationship, as they threaten all relationships at sometime or another, remember to focus on what is right between you, not only the part that seems wrong. In this way, you can ride out the times when clouds drift across the face of the sun in your lives, remembering that, just because you may lose sight of it for a moment, does not mean the sun has gone away. And, if each of you takes total responsibility for the quality of your life together, it will be marked by abundance and delight.

You may now kiss!

The Affirmation

We know not what the future may bring into the lives of Bride and Groom, but we believe that together they may be equal to the needs of their days to come. May they find patience in time of stress, strength in time of weakness, courage in time of discouragement, vision in time of doubt, and, in all time, a growing love.

We who are here present, and those who are absent, thinking of these two people, hope that the inspiration of this hour will not be forgotten. May they continue to love one another forever.

We will close with this Native American Wedding Prayer
Now you will feel no rain, for each of you will be shelter for the other.
Now you will feel no cold, for each of you will be warmth to the other.
Now you are two persons, but there is only one life before you.
Go now to your dwelling to enter into the days of your life together.
And may your days be good, and long upon the earth.

Ladies and gentleman, I introduce to you for the first time, Mr. and Mrs. Groom (or however you would like to be introduced)!

Recessional

CEREMONY EXAMPLE NUMBER FIVE

We are gathered here to join this man and this woman in marriage, an estate made honorable by the faithful keeping of good men and women in all times. It is therefore not to be entered into lightly or unadvisedly, but reverently, discreetly, and soberly.

In marriage, two persons turn to each other in search of a greater fulfillment than either can achieve alone. Marriage is a going forth, a bold step into the future; it is risking what we are for the sake of what we can be.

Only in giving oneself and sharing with another can the mysterious process of growth take place. Only in loyalty and devotion bestowed upon another can that which is eternal in life emerge and be known. Two among us, who have stood apart, come now, in our presence, to declare their love and to be united in marriage.

One poet has written of marriage:
You were born together, and together you shall be...
But let there be spaces in your togetherness, and let the winds of the heavens dance between you.
Love one another, but make not a bond of love...
Sing and dance together and be joyous but let each one of you be alone, even as the strings of a lute are alone though they quiver with the same music.
Give your hearts, but not into each other's keeping...
And stand together, yet not too near together:
For the pillars of the temple stand apart, and the oak tree and the cypress grow not in each other's shadow.

(Kahlil Gibran, The Prophet)

Marriage is an institution ordained of the very laws of our being, for the happiness and welfare of humanity. To be true, this outward ceremony must be but a symbol of that which is inner and real, a sacred union of hearts the church may bless and the state make legal, but that neither can create nor annul.

Marriage is not meant for happiness alone, but for the discipline and enrichment of character. To this end there must be a consecration of each to the other, and of both to the noblest purposes of life.

It is in this spirit that we believe you have both come here today.

Optional Personal Vows by Groom
Optional Personal Vows by Bride

Groom will you have this woman to be your wedded wife, to live together in marriage, will you love her, comfort her, honor and keep her, in sickness and health, in sorrow and in joy, so long as you both shall live?

Answer: "I will!"

Bride will you have this man to be your wedded husband, to live together in marriage, will you love him, comfort him, honor and keep him, in sickness and health, in sorrow and in joy, so long as you both shall live?

Answer: "I will!"

Join your right hands.

(Cued) I Groom take you Bride, to be my wedded wife, to have and to hold, from this day forward, for better and for worse, for richer and for poorer, in sickness and health, to love and to cherish, so long as we both shall live.

(Cued) I Bride take you Groom, to be my wedded husband, to have and to hold, from this day forward, for better and for worse, for richer and for poorer, in sickness and health, to love and to cherish, so long as we both shall live.

(Officiant to man)
What pledge do you offer that you will keep these vows?

Answer: "This ring!"

(Officiant to Bride)
Do you accept this in token of the same?

Answer: "I do!"

You will then place the ring on her finger and repeat after me.

(Cued) Groom: "With this ring, I marry you."

(Officiant to woman)
What pledge do you offer that you will keep these vows?

Answer: "This ring!"

(Officiant to Groom)
Do you accept this in token of the same?

Answer: "I do!"

You will then place the ring on his finger and repeat after me.

(Cued) Bride: "With this ring, I marry you."

For as much as these two persons have solemnly promised to live together in wedlock, and have engaged and pledged themselves by the giving and receiving of the marriage rings, I therefore, ministering in the name of these high ideals, and with the authority vested in me by the state of Texas, do pronounce you now husband and wife.

You may now kiss!

Benediction
Let us pray. May love bless this union and make its days increase constantly in joy and satisfaction. May the blessings of those around you attend you and keep you together always, in understanding, tenderness and love. Amen

Ladies and gentleman, I introduce to you for the first time, Mr. and Mrs. Groom (or however you would like to be introduced)!

CEREMONY EXAMPLE
NUMBER SIX

Officiant:

Good evening, and welcome to the ceremony that will unite Groom and Bride in marriage. We gather here today to celebrate their union, and to honor their commitment to not just gazing at one another, but to looking outward together in the same direction. Today Groom and Bride proclaim their love to the world, and we rejoice with them and for them.

In marriage, we give ourselves freely and generously into the hands of the one we love, and in doing so, each of us receives the love and trust of the other as our most precious gift. But even as that gift is shared by two people who are in love, it also touches the friends and family members who in various ways support and contribute to the relationship. All of you are Groom and Bride's community, and each of you has played some part in bringing them to this moment. This is why gathering as a community is such an important part of a wedding ceremony. Because Groom and Bride are now taking a new form as a married couple, and in this form, they become part of their community in a new way.

(NOTE TO COUPLES: If you want to insert something personal, such as a favorite poem or song, or a statement made to one another, this is the spot for it).

Groom and Bride, we are here to remember and rejoice with you, and to recount with one another that it is love that guides us on our path, and to celebrate as you begin this journey together. It is in this spirit that you have come here to today to exchange these vows.

Vows

Groom, repeat after me:
I Groom take you Bride to be my wife/
You are the other half of me,
and with your love I am complete/
I humbly give you my hand and my heart/
as a sanctuary of warmth and peace/
and pledge my faith and love to you.

Bride, repeat after me:
I Bride take you Groom to be my husband/
You are the other half of me,
and with your love I am complete/
I humbly give you my hand and my heart/
as a sanctuary of warmth and peace/
and pledge my faith and love to you.

Rings

Wedding rings are made precious by our wearing of them. Your rings say that even in your uniqueness you have chosen to be bound together. Let your rings also be a sign that love has substance as well as soul, a present as well as a past, and that, despite its occasional sorrows, love is a circle of happiness, wonder, and delight.

Groom, take Bride's ring and put it on her finger, and repeat after me:
Just as this circle is without end, my love for you is eternal/
Just as it is made of indestructible substance/my commitment to you will never fail/With this ring I take you to be my trusted confidante and partner for life.

Bride, put the ring on Groom's finger and repeat after me:
Just as this circle is without end, my love for you is eternal/
Just as it is made of indestructible substance/my commitment to you will never fail/With this ring I take you to be my trusted confidante and partner for life.

Pronouncement

Inasmuch as you have consented together in this ceremony to live in wedlock and have sealed your vows in the presence of this assembly and by the giving of these rings, it gives me great pleasure to pronounce that you are husband and wife.

Groom, you may kiss your bride!

Ladies and gentleman, I introduce to you for the first time, Mr. and Mrs. Groom (or however you would like to be introduced)!

ADDITIONAL CEREMONY ITEMS

Another Ceremony of the Candles

Bride and Groom, the two separate candles symbolize your separate lives, separate families and separate sets of friends. I ask that each of you take one of the lit candles and that together you light the center candle. The individual candles represent your lives before today. Lighting the center candle represents that your two lives are now joined to one light, and represents the joining together of your two families and sets of friends to one.

Wine Cup Ceremony

(This ceremony may be used in place of the Unity Candle.)
The years of life are as a cup of wine poured out for you to drink. The cup of life contains within it the sweet wine of happiness, joy, hope and delight. The same cup, at times, holds the bitter wine of disappointment, sorrow, grief, and despair. Those who drink deeply of life invite the full range of experiences into their being. This cup is symbolic of the pledges you have made to one another to share together the fullness of life. As you drink from this cup, you acknowledge to one another that your lives, until this moment separate, have become one vessel into which all your sorrows and joys, all your hopes and fears, all you dreams and dreads, will be poured, and from which you will find mutual sustenance. Many days you will sit at the same table and eat and drink together.

Drink now, and may the cup of your lives be sweet and full to overflowing. (Present glass to Groom, he will sip and pass it to Bride.)

10

Nice Touches: Additional Ceremony Ideas

o o o o o o o o o o o o o o o o o o o o o o o o o o o o o o o o

My love for you is a journey;
Starting at forever,
And ending at never.

—Anonymous

Melissa and Jeff knew they wanted to do something different in their wedding. They planned all of the details but still felt there was something missing. Jeff's uncle had played a significant role is his early childhood. They wanted Uncle Tim to have a role within this very special day. Uncle Tim was asked to honor the couple with a reading of his choice. Uncle Tim performed wonderfully and the reading was beautiful.

There are many things you can do within your ceremony to include others and to personalize your ceremony. These examples are not intended to be all-inclusive but instead should serve to start you thinking of options you might have within the ceremony.

Readings

Many couples will include readings in their wedding ceremonies. You probably noticed within the ceremony examples in the preceding chapter there were several opportunities to have special readings recited. Most commonly in our culture these readings are from the Bible. Because of this I have included two appendices with the most popular of biblical readings for weddings.

However, if you do not desire readings from the Bible, I encourage you to use any reading that holds meaning for the two of you. There may be a favorite poem that is reminiscent of your love. Shakespeare's sonnets are often used in weddings and are very well received. You may also think about some of the lyrics from your favorite songs. The best songs are poems put to music. It might be appropriate for your favorite lyrics to serve as readings within your wedding.

Music

Music is another wonderful avenue through which to personalize your ceremony. Your wedding does not necessarily have to follow along with traditional dictates when it comes to music. You may want to enter hearing Vivaldi, Bach, Pachelbel, the wedding march, and Ave Maria for candle lighting. But then again you may not.

I have assisted many couples who have marched out to the musical strains of their favorite rock band. Others have looked soulfully into each other's eyes while a friend sings their favorite country and western song. These musical selections were appropriate for these couples and added a certain amount of genuineness to the event.

Music is usually very personal for individuals and couples. The music you choose for your wedding can help your personalities shine through. Your choices may also show reverence for the wedding traditions of our society. Either way you will have important choices to make that will influence the mood and feeling of your wedding.

Involving Children

Some couples desire to involve children in their ceremonies. Most often the children serve as ring boys and flower girls. There are a couple of things you might consider when involving children in your ceremony.

First of all, does the child want to participate? We often think of the little ones in a miniature tuxedo or dress as irresistibly cute. This is true much of the time. There are other times when adults have merely bestowed upon a child the responsibility of playing an almost adult role in this big event. Sometimes the child does not want to do this. I have seen many children display poor behavior during the ceremony as a way to help let the adults realize that this was not *their* idea.

Also, what is the age and temperament of the child? Again, children may look cute all dolled up, but are they able to handle the responsibility that comes with their wedding position? I think many couples have a gut-level feeling as to whether or not they should have children involved in their wedding. Sometimes they acknowledge that feeling and other times they choose to ignore it.

It may also be the case that whatever the young one does in the ceremony is okay by the two of you. Children will often present us with comic relief during a wedding ceremony. I once heard the story of a young boy, about three years old, who was to bring up the wedding rings on a pillow. Each step he took up the aisle was accompanied by a great "roar!" People could not help but laugh. When the young boy reached his father, the best man, he was asked why he was making the animal noises. The boy replied, "Because I am the ring bear!"

The Family Medallion

Children from previous relationships are rightfully becoming integral parts of some couple's weddings. One of the most beautiful ways of doing this is through the use of a Family Medallion. The Family Medallion is a symbol using three circles incorporated within a larger circle. The inner circles represent the mother, father, and the child. The outer circle represents the entire family.

Dr. Roger Coleman has done a wonderful job in bringing the Family Medallion, and its ceremony, to thousands of people. To find out more about the Family Medallion go to the website (http://www.familymedallion.com).

Adventure Weddings?

Another avenue some couples take is incorporating adventure within their wedding. Weddings can be extremely fun events. Fun weddings these days are taking many shapes. One of the ways couples are incorporating fun, in a daring sort of way, is adventure weddings. What is an adventure wedding, you ask? It is a wedding that has incorporated a component of risk to it. Very few couples are doing this but it definitely gives the wedding a completely different feel and experience. There are three types of adventure weddings that immediately come to mind. These are: underwater weddings, mountaintop weddings, and (yes) the skydiving wedding.

Why would anyone want to get married like this? I believe there are several reasons to have an adventure wedding. First and foremost, an adventure wedding tells others who you are and, to some extent, what you are about as a couple. Couples who have shared a great deal through their SCUBA diving, for example, or met through a dive trip might want to make a public statement of sorts regarding how this activity has played a role in their lives. People who enjoy the great outdoors and feel more at home in a tent than a country club may want to marry at a lake or on a mountaintop. And folks who are crazy enough to jump out of a perfectly good airplane may want to extend the free falling sensation to their nuptial bliss.

Another reason couples may choose to incorporate adventure in their nuptials is that they want their wedding to be like no other. Because the tradition of weddings is so strong, we often wind up having weddings that appear to be very similar. While the bride and groom often know the intricacies of their event, the average wedding observer will see many of the same things at all of the weddings they attend. At some point it becomes difficult to discern whether you attended cousin Julie's or aunt Pat's wedding because they begin to look so similar. The adventure wedding does not suffer from this dilemma.

There are a few problems you might encounter when planning an adventure wedding. First of all, you most likely cannot have a wedding for 200 on the top of a mountain or underwater. Thus, participation of family and friends may be greatly limited. Also, you might have difficulty locating a minister who will perform the ceremony. You may have to search high and low (no pun intended) to find a member of the clergy willing to go to the lengths required for an adventure wedding. Finally, you must contend with the whims of the weather. Rain might put a real damper on an adventure wedding that has no back-up plan.

My biggest suggestion for adventure weddings is that couples have two ceremonies. Have your adventure wedding first with your closest friends. Or, depending upon where you get married, you may just want the officiant and any required witnesses to be present. You will definitely want to have someone take pictures at this event. Follow this up with a second ceremony for your entire group of friends and family. In this way you will have the wedding that you want and a ceremony in which others can participate. You can keep the adventure wedding a secret or proudly display photographs of your adventure wedding.

The closest thing that I have come to participating in an adventure wedding was a wonderful hot air balloon wedding. We met on a day that was almost too windy to launch the balloon. We spoke of their soaring love as the balloon took them into the air and the surrounding white fluffy clouds. The couple then floated into a beautiful sky near the time of sunset. This wonderful couple had also purchased a balloon ride for my wife and me. We took off in the balloon for a wonderful experience we will never forget.

It is true that adventure weddings are not for everyone. The time honored somber tradition of the wedding day is something with which most folks do not want to trifle. However, there may be a few of you who just may want to do something a bit off the beaten path. It is for you that the adventure wedding beckons. Remember, however, that weddings are public events in which your families and friends *expect* to participate. By having two ceremonies everyone can have what they want and desire.

11

What to Do When Things Go Wrong

○ ○
The greatest weakness of most humans
Is their hesitancy to tell others,
How much they love them
While they're alive.

—*O.A. Battista*

Kara and Lance planned for almost a year in order to have the perfect wedding. They constructed checklists, signed vendor contracts, and knew that everything was in place for their perfect day.

But the day was not perfect. The driver for the bakery had been in a serious accident on his way to deliver the bride and groom cakes. Kara was initially devastated. How could they have a reception without a cake? She then seemed to suddenly realize that a man had been seriously injured and that maybe the cakes were not as important as the delivery man's health.

Something had gone wrong the day of their perfect wedding. But Kara and Lance realized that it was not the cakes that were important. They planned well but there had been a glitch. They were able to let go, right then and there, of their need for the day to be perfect.

Not everyone is able to do this. I have seen brides cry because any number of little things had gone wrong on their wedding day. No matter how much we plan and prepare, weddings are rarely perfect. If you are able to be comfortable with this idea of possible imperfection today, your wedding will be a breeze.

The Rehearsal

One of the ways we can get closer to the perfect wedding is by rehearsing. The rehearsal will show the bridal party what to do, allow the ushers to understand their roles more fully, and work out any last minute kinks in the ceremony.

The way I conduct a rehearsal is to have everyone start by standing where they will stand during the ceremony. That way they know how to hit their mark, so to speak, when time for the ceremony arrives. The bride will usually have specific ideas of how the bridal party should stand during the wedding.

I will then go through the highlights of the ceremony. We will then exit out and proceed back in and go through the ceremony again. After marching out again most people feel perfectly fine about their role in the ceremony.

In most rehearsals I am asked about the order of the processional (walking in) and recessional (walking out). The easiest way to remember this is that the bride is the traditionally the focal point of a wedding. The bride's family is traditionally closest to her in proximity. To accomplish this closeness the bride's family comes in after the groom's so as to be nearer to her.

So, during the processional the groom's grandparents will be escorted up the aisle first followed by the bride's. The groom's mother will be escorted up the aisle, may light one of the Unity Candle tapers, and then followed by the bride's mother who may also light a candle.

When we march out it is opposite of the processional. The bride's mother, in order to be closest to her daughter is escorted out first, either by an usher or the bride's father. The bride's mother is followed by the groom's parents, the bride's grandparents, and finally the groom's grandparents walk back down the aisle.

Work closely with your ushers in this matter. They are often a bit overwhelmed by who goes where and when. You can help them by modifying the Review Table below and incorporating family names.

In Review

Order of Processional	*Order of Recessional*
Grandparents of Groom	Bride and Groom
Grandparents of Bride	Best Man and Maid/Matron of Honor
Mother of Groom	Attendants
Mother of Bride	Parents of Bride
Bridal Attendants in Reverse Order	Parents of Groom
(Men and Officiant are generally already in	Grandparents of Bride
place at front)	Grandparents of Groom
Bride and Escort	Minister

Additional Rehearsal Tips

Smile!

I think it is very important for people to "practice" smiling during the rehearsal. Mothers, fathers, bride, groom, wedding party, ushers—everybody should practice smiling during the rehearsal so that it is a more natural act during the ceremony. People should be smiling because the wedding is a joyous event. People will often not smile because they are nervous. However, when people in the ceremony do not smile folks may think they disapprove of the wedding. So, smile and let people know you are happy with the marriage.

Of course, crying at a wedding is perfectly acceptable. Most people will assume the tears to be those of joy. There is nothing more beautiful to me than the tears shed by both bride and groom and their families during their wedding ceremony. I often get choked up as well.

Do not arrive late to the rehearsal.

Showing up late is a big problem for wedding rehearsals. People most often have wonderful excuses as to why they were late. However, for this occasion I would ask people to make special arrangements so they will arrive on time, or better yet early, for the rehearsal. Some brides have resorted to telling rehearsal participants to arrive 15 or even 30 minutes early in order to eliminate tardiness. What is even more worrisome is when the bride shows up late to the rehearsal. There may be legitimate reasons for tardiness in many circumstances but try your best to be on time.

Ask for limited talking during the rehearsal.

This is difficult to do. Many times people will not have seen one another in quite some time and it is natural to want to catch up. I usually tell folks that the sooner we can get through the rehearsal the sooner we can get to the rehearsal dinner and visit with one another. If people are talking it is difficult for them to listen. If they do not listen they will not know what to do on the big day. If they do not know what to do at the wedding the rehearsal has been a failure. Remaining quiet during the 30–45 minutes required for a rehearsal, while possibly difficult, should not be too much to ask of your friends and family.

During the Ceremony Tips

Here are just a few things that I ask couples to think about with regard to the ceremony. My hope is these tips will be helpful to you as well.

Do what is comfortable.

Many times couples will be so intent on doing everything "right" they become entangled in the most intricate of details. Couples will often ask, when do we hold hands, should we do this or that, and a host of other worries. I encourage couples to be as comfortable as they can in front of this large group of people who have come to see them get married. If you want to hold hands, then please do. Hand the bouquet over when it seems to be the proper time to do so. I do, however, ask that couples refrain from kissing until the appointed time. A good officiant will be able to speak in such a way that only the couple can hear instructions or directions during the ceremony. The officiant will also be able to project his or her voice during the ceremony for all others to hear. Let the officiant help you.

Look deeply into one another's eyes.

Many times a bride or groom will look at me when repeating his or her vows. This is quite natural to do as most people in our culture usually make eye contact with the person to whom they are speaking. I ask couples to look at one another during the repeating of vows. After all, they are marrying one another…not me! I tell the bride and groom that I will take the vows slowly and in small fragments so as not to get far ahead of them. If they look at me during the reciting of vows I immediately begin to look at their partner. They will often then look deeply into their partner's eyes as they promise to have and to hold.

Let the rings fall.

Although this rarely occurs, there have been times when the Best Man drops the ring when attempting to give the bride's ring to the groom. The same has occurred, of course, when the Maid/Matron of Honor has attempted to give the bride the groom's ring. I suggest the attendant put the ring on their little finger and allow the bride or groom to take it from them rather than have it dropped in their hand. However, if the ring does indeed fall, I ask the attendant to take responsibility for retrieving the ring. Neither the bride nor groom should be chasing the ring wherever it may have been dropped. There have even been times when the Best Man and groom have butted heads when both were trying to retrieve the ring at the same time. I tell them to let the ring fall and then the attendant will locate the ring and bring it back so it can be used in the ceremony.

Reception Tips

For many people the reception is the highlight of the wedding day. No matter how beautiful the ceremony was, it is now time to say hello to your guests and have a wonderful time. The reception should have a wonderful flow and pace. This flow and pace is often difficult for the bride and groom to discern as they are so engrossed in the goings on of the reception. Believe it or not, guests can become more than a little bored at a reception where the events do not flow well.

I suggest to couples that they work on a timeline. If you have a wedding coordinator she or he should do this for you automatically. If you do not have a coordinator the disc jockey can often serve as your Master of Ceremonies to announce each piece of the reception puzzle. You may also ask a friend to be responsible for keeping you on time.

The following outline should serve only as a guide. You may change the sequence of events, the allotted time, or delete items you would rather not do. You may, of course add things I have not listed.

Immediately Following Ceremony (30–45 minutes)

- Formal photograph's taken of Bride and Groom, family and wedding party

- Guest may enjoy the beverage of their choice at reception location

Arrival and Dances (30 minutes)

- Master of Ceremonies announces wedding party (traditional order is: groom's parents, bride's parents, flower girl and ring bearer, bridesmaids escorted by ushers, maid of honor escorted by best man, Bride and Groom).

- Bride and Groom's first dance

- Toasting (traditional order is: Best Man, Fathers [groom's then bride's], Groom, Bride, Friends and Relatives, Maid/Matron of Honor, Mothers (groom's then bride's), Anyone else wishing to toast

Let's Eat! (60–90 minutes)

- Dinner served

- Cut cake

- Special dances in order: Bride with father, then Groom with mother, and Wedding party dance.

- Everybody dancing

Some fun stuff (30minutes)

- Bouquet toss

- Garter toss

- Last dance of Bride and Groom

- Grand exit

This outline should give you an idea of how your reception might be structured. There is a great deal to do in three or so hours. Get help in order to keep things on track and your guests involved. With a little planning you have the ability to have one of the best receptions your guests will attend.

You will find that with a little preparation and practice few things will go wrong in your wedding. You will have done all that you can to have the closest thing possible to the perfect wedding.

12

After the Wedding

o o o o o o o o o o o o o o o o o o o o o o o o o o o o o o o o o o
The person who tries to live alone will not succeed as a human
being.
His heart withers if it does not answer another heart.
His mind shrinks away if he hears only the echoes of his
own thoughts and finds no other inspiration.

—Pearl S. Buck

Theresa and Richard were just getting over their excitement of all that was their wedding. There had been so much to do, they had so much fun, the honeymoon was spectacular, and now they were exhausted. They looked at each other and wondered what would come next in their lives.

After the wedding you may find there to be a certain lull in your life. Planning a wedding can entirely consume your life for a period of time. It is perfectly normal to feel overwhelmed throughout the planning process and then to feel a sort of lull or low point at some time after the big day. There is no longer the rush to meet wedding vendors, drive to reception locations, or plan your ceremony. This feeling should soon pass as you are about to begin your married life together.

My hope for you is that you have a long and happy marriage. So, I just want to briefly offer a few tips as you begin this journey. I believe you two will have many choices regarding your marriage. I ask that you make a commitment to choose wisely.

Your Love Will Change

First, I feel it is my duty to let you know that your love *will* change with time. The fact of the matter is the way you love one another today will change in five years and will go through several different stages throughout your married life. I tell you this not to disillusion but to educate. If you know your love will change it does not become frightening when it begins to happen. In fact, one of the major reasons the United States has such a high divorce rate is people believe they are *supposed* to feel the same way about their spouse after several years of marriage. Said in another way, many people believe if the honeymoon feeling is gone, something must be wrong.

I am here to tell you it is perfectly normal and expected by marriage counselors, that your love for one another will change. All relationships travel through ups and downs. Couples who are able to stay together through the down times, knowing that an up time will follow, will have a long marriage. Promise yourselves not to give up when it seems difficult.

I believe that many couples who divorce give up too easily. They have seen divorce modeled in their family and their friends and believe they too must succumb to divorce. As long as there is no violence or addiction in the relationship, there is potential for the relationship to improve. I virtually guarantee it. You must love one another for better and for worse.

A great deal of marriage research demonstrates that the majority of divorces are within "low conflict" couples. These couples do not fight severely, there is no addiction, and there are no extramarital affairs. Their love has simply (and normally) changed. They do not understand that the honeymoon always comes to an end and they must now work at their relationship. They thought their love was different.

Do not let this happen to you. You have been forewarned! With greater relationship knowledge you two do not have to be another statistic. Make the choice to acknowledge your love will change over time.

Take Responsibility

You must also take responsibility for keeping your marriage fresh. I tell couples they should continue to date throughout their married lives. We most often fall in love with the person we date. We take great pains to be on our best behavior when we date. We go out of our way not to hurt the other person with our words when we date. So, it makes sense to continue to date in your marriage.

Few couples really take this advice to heart. We all get into ruts and routines in our married lives. We take the other person for granted and often believe our partner to be ultimately responsible for our own happiness. As the saying goes, we often hurt the ones we love.

Do not allow the plethora of excuses get in the way of keeping your marriage alive. Read positive books about marriage (see my bookstore at www.marriage-education.net), make a specific night of the week your date night, and refuse to allow your relationship go stale.

Remember the words from ceremony example number four, "[Y]ou can ride out the times when clouds drift across the face of the sun in your lives, remembering that, just because you may lose sight of it for a moment, does not mean the sun has gone away. And, if each of you *takes total responsibility* for the quality of your life together, it will be marked by abundance and delight."

You must together agree that your relationship will remain the priority of your lives. We all have choices to make each day. You have the ability, even the power, to choose your relationship priority. Choose to make it a very high priority indeed.

Create Rituals

Some couples begin couple and family rituals after marriage as a way to keep the marriage alive. A ritual can be anything from making Fridays movie night to visiting in-laws every Sunday. Rituals give us a sense of comfort and reassure us that things are going well. Rituals are things enjoyed by both people in the marriage. Rituals differ from ruts and routines because of the pleasure that is associated with your ritual.

I suggest couples subscribe to Marriage Magazine (http://www. marriagemagazine.org) or some other similar publication. Each time the magazine arrives make it a ritual to sit down together and spend time going through the magazine together. Choose which articles you will read and which your partner will read. Give each other reports of what you read and how you two might possibly incorporate some new things into your relationship. Every time the magazine arrives in your mailbox you will be reminded that your relationship is a priority.

As I counsel couples who are in marital distress I often find the couple believes there is little time left for the relationship. Too many things are in the way and take time away from the relationship. Again, you must make the choices to have a marriage that lasts. Make the choice to create fun and marriage enriching rituals into your relationship.

You might also think about promising to attend a seminar or workshop once a year that focuses on marriage. While perhaps this is not a ritual per se, it is something that you could build into your life as a couple and something you could each look forward to each year. It is also another reminder that you have chosen to make your marriage a priority and give you a yearly opportunity to focus on one another.

An excellent book you might read about creating rituals is *The Intentional Family: Simple Rituals to Strengthen Family Ties* by William J. Doherty. There are also many ritual examples on the website of Coalition for Marriage, Family, and Couples Education (http://www.smartmarriages.com).

Get Professional Help

In the event that one or both of you are having difficulties in your marriage I ask that you promise one another to get professional help. It may be the person who assisted you with premarital counseling is also a licensed counselor. It may be a counselor that a friend of yours recommends. See a counselor with whom you both feel comfortable. If you do not find the level of comfort you desire with the counselor then find another one. There are plenty of counselors available to assist you in your marriage. Find the one with whom you can relate.

Also, be sure the counselor is "pro-marriage." As odd as it may sound, there are several researchers who have found marriage counseling to be damaging to a relationship. This is most often due to the counselor's belief that people should do whatever is needed in order to find self-fulfillment. If this means divorce, well at least you tried, they say.

I say baloney! In your wedding the two of you have said you will work through the good times and the bad. You said that together you are stronger than you are apart. You exchanged rings and told everyone who would listen that you loved one another and that you would remain committed to each other. I ask that you do what you said you would do in your wedding ceremony. When you are in need of professional help, and the counselor is pro-marriage, you have much better odds in getting through to the other side of this difficulty.

And speaking of odds, you may have heard it said that it is important for marriage to be a 50/50 partnership. I do not believe this is true. You must each give 100% to your marriage. If you feel you are giving more to your marriage than your partner, say 70/30, you merely wind up keeping score. If you both feel you are giving everything you can to the relationship then everybody wins.

I believe that your marriage can last. You may be one of the couples who have very few problems at all in their marriage. But if problems do arise I hope you will look for the sun in your lives when times seem hard. I will promise you the amount of money spent on professional counseling (check your healthcare benefit) will be far less than the monetary cost of a divorce, not to mention the emotional cost to each other, your children, and family. Make the choice to get professional help if needed and stay married forever!

13

Concluding Thoughts

o o o o o o o o o o o o o o o o o o o o o o o o o o o o o o o o

Life without love is like a tree
Without blossom and fruit.

—*Khalil Gibran*

If you have not drawn anything else from this book I hope it is that you have a great deal of control over your wedding. You have choices to make in vendors, in ceremony wording, even in the guests you will invite. The tasks can seem overwhelming but you are indeed up to the task. This book has hopefully addressed some things you have already thought about and many others you may have not.

My hope for this little book was to get you thinking about these choices. The book was meant to be read fairly quickly and to give you some ideas of how to proceed. I have often heard brides say, something to the effect of, "I have never been married and I just don't know where to start." My hope is that you now know where to start. I also hope you will take and use the ideas that I have learned and use the ones that make most sense to you. Delete those ideas that do not feel quite right to you. Make your day special and then proceed to make your marriage special.

There are literally dozens of books in print that will assist you with your wedding planning. I appreciate the fact that you have chosen this one.

If you have any suggestions for future editions I hope you will contact me. I would like the book to be even more relevant and helpful to couples. Feel free to contact me with questions through either of my websites.

I wish you luck, I wish you love, and I wish you the best wedding ever!

ADDITIONAL READING

A Bride's Book of Wedding Traditions (1995) by A.H. Stewart. Hearst Books: New York

A Ceremony to Remember (2000) by Mart Younkin. Love Notes Publishing: Richardson, TX

Alternative Weddings: An Essential Guide for Creating Your Own Ceremonies (1997) by Jane Ross-MacDonald. Taylor Publishing: Dallas.

Joining Hands and Hearts: Interfaith, Intercultural Wedding Celebrations (2003) by Rev. Susanna Stefanachi Macomb. Fireside: New York.

The Intentional Family: Simple Rituals to Strengthen Family Ties (1999) by William J. Doherty. Avon: New York.

Weddings for Dummies (1997) by Blum, Fisher, & Kaiser. John Wiley & Sons: New York

Weddings: The Magic of Creating Your Own Ceremony by (1999) by Basayne & Janowitz. Bookpartners, Inc: Newberg, OR

10 Great Dates to Revitalize Your Marriage (1997) by David Arp and Claudia Arp. Zondervan Publishing House: Grand Rapids, MI.

A FEW INTERNET RESOURCES

Rev. Dr. Russell K. Elleven   http://www.marriage-education.net

Smart Marriages   http://www.smartmarriages.com

The Family Medallion   http://www.familymedallion.com

Ultimate Wedding   http://www.ultimatewedding.com

International Association of Pastoral Counselors   http://www.iapcinc.org

American Association of Pastoral Counselors   http://www.aapc.org

American Counseling Association   http://www.counseling.org

National Board of Certified Counselors   http://www.nbcc.org

American Assoc. for Marriage & Family Therapy   http://www.aamft.org

Marriage Magazine   http://www.marriagemagazine.org

APPENDICES

APPENDIX A
BEST MAN DUTIES

The Best Man is:

- *The Clothing coordinator*—the Best Man should make sure all rented clothing has been ordered. Most likely the Best Man will be responsible for picking up and returning the clothing to the shop for all of the male wedding party members. Make sure too that all accessories (i.e., ties, gloves, ascots, cufflinks, etc.) are received and how to use them so you can assist others.

- *The Usher Coordinator*—make sure you understand the duties and responsibilities of the ushers. You should be able to help them remember who to seat where and when (see more below).

- *The Bachelor Party Coordinator*—traditionally the Best Man has coordinated this event. Dating back to Roman times, the party has been seen as the final fling of a man before he is "tied down" to one woman. Be cautious here. While the event should be memorable, you do not want the bride to despise you for the rest of your life because of a bachelor party. If you envision a raucous evening of drinking, plan the event a week in advance of the ceremony. You do not want the groom to be physically ill on his wedding day. Take necessary precautions like renting a limousine or having a designated driver. Thankfully the trend is moving away from these types of parties and towards entire affairs built around sporting themes such as golf. Use your imagination and be safe!

- *The Gift Giver*—collect money from the ushers and groomsmen to buy a gift from you all. Make sure to allow time for engraving or monogramming if necessitated by the gift. Usually you can make the presentation with all the men at hand prior to the ceremony. Think of what you will say in advance. Make the occasion memorable for your relationship with the groom is soon likely to change. Additionally, you will be a great hit if you personally have roses or champagne delivered to the couple's hotel room or cruise line cabin!

- *Personal Assistant*—you are basically the valet or servant of the groom. You will help him in arranging the honeymoon, packing for the trip, making sure he has the wedding license and a passport if necessary, getting the luggage to the airport and checking it in, giving him the claim checks, etc. Whew!

- *Time Keeper*—you should make sure the groom is always on time. Assist him in getting dressed, to the ceremony location, leaving the reception (with the bride), and to the dock or airport with time to spare.

- *Money Keeper*—it is usually the responsibility of the Best Man to see that the officiant is paid. However, the fee is most often given to the Best Man by the groom. Make sure you are aware of the arrangement in advance of the wedding ceremony. Wedding officiants often do not want to embarrass anyone by having to ask for their fee.

- *Transportation Guru*—you may need to drive the groom to the ceremony location. You may be asked to drive the couple from the ceremony to the reception if chauffeured limousines are not used. Airport runs are also not uncommon. If they are using their own "get-away car" the Best Man will often see that the vehicle is appropriately decorated. Use precautions so that paint is not damaged or that embarrassing sayings or phrases are not used.

- *Speechmaker*—you will toast the new couple at the reception. This responsibility takes time and preparation and for many is a gut wrenching experience (you may refer to the toasting tips in this book). Remember this: You do not have to be an accomplished orator to make a successful wedding toast.

- *Master of ceremonies*—be prepared to introduce the wedding party at the reception and to announce the dances that traditionally accompany the reception. Most often these duties are left to the band leader or disc jockey. Find out about this task in advance.

- *Dancer*—you will usually have the fourth dance with the bride. She will dance with the groom, her father, her father-in-law, and then you. If you are blessed with two left feet you may want to find out what kind of dance is expected and take a lesson or two.

APPENDIX B
MAID/MATRON OF HONOR DUTIES

The Maid of Honor is:

- **The Dressing Attendant**—traditionally you are asked to assist the bride as she dresses for the big event. WARNING: This is sometimes a very stressful time for the bride. Be understanding and gentle with the bride during this time.

- **Dress Caretaker**—there will be times during the ceremony when you should make sure the bride's dress looks its best. You may want to "fluff" the dress after the bride takes her place for the ceremony, returns from lighting the Unity Candle, or during the taking of pictures.

- **The Bouquet Holder**—at some point during the ceremony the bride will hand her bouquet to you. You will probably learn the time this is to occur during the rehearsal. However, be ready for the bouquet to come your way at any time in order to provide the bride with more flexibility.

- **Holder of the Ring**—you will, most likely, be holding the groom's ring until such time as the couple exchanges wedding bands. Again, the rehearsal should make this duty perfectly clear. Just be alert and you will have no problems with this responsibility.

- **The Dressing Attendant: Part II**—usually the maid or matron of honor assists the bride when she changes clothes to leave for the honeymoon. This is a great time to say goodbye to your formerly single friend.

APPENDIX C
USHER DUTIES

The Ushers Should:

Boutonniere—pin the flower of your left lapel. It is often easier to have someone do this for you.

In Advance Part I—find out if you are responsible for escorting in all guests or just the grandparents and parents. Hint: Ask the bride. She will most often be glad to make sure you know her preference.

Know Your Right from Your Left—if you are escorting all guests, tradition asks that you seat guests of the bride on the left and groom on the right. It may help to imagine where the bride and groom stand during the ceremony. Their guests will sit on that same side. This tradition is being used less and less so make sure you know what the bride wants to do.

In Advance Part II—make sure you know specifically the grandparent and/ or parent you will be escorting. Most likely, you will escort these same dignitaries up and down the aisle.

Know the Order—ushers should memorize this order:Before the ceremony:First—Groom's Grandparents
Second—Bride's Grandparents
Third—Groom's Parents (Mother may light Unity Candle taper)
Forth—Bride's Mother (may light Unity Candle taper)After the ceremony (reverse order):First—Bride's parents
Second—Groom's Parents
Third—Bride's Grandparents
Fourth—Groom's Grandparents

APPENDIX D
PROCESSIONAL/RECESSIONAL ORDER

TYPICAL ORDER OF PROCESSIONAL

- Grandparents of Groom

- Grandparents of Bride

- Parents of Groom (mother may light Unity Candle taper)

- Mother of Bride—if father is escorting bride (mother may light Unity Candle taper)

- Groom's party entrance

- Bridal party (reverse order)

- Ring Bearer (if applicable)

- Flower Girl (if applicable)

- Bride (and escort)

TYPICAL ORDER OF RECESSIONAL

- New Husband and Wife!

- Ring Bearer/Flower Girl (if applicable)

- Best Man and Maid/Matron of Honor

- Attendants

- Parents of Bride

- Parents of Groom

- Grandparents of Bride

- Grandparents of Groom

- Minister

BIBLICAL APPENDICES

It is becoming increasingly true that our society is less familiar with the scriptures of the Judaic and Christian religions. While I am certainly not here to bemoan this circumstance, I thought it might be helpful to outline some of the most commonly used Old and New Testament Bible verses for wedding ceremonies. It is becoming ever more common that wedding party members are being asked to increase their participation through the reading of scripture during the ceremony.

Keep in mind as you read these verses and phrases of the Old and New Testaments that they are taken from the New Revised Standard Version of the Bible. Some couples and officiants continue to desire the Old English version of scripture as found in the King James Version of the Bible because of its regal sound. You probably will want to check this assumption out with the couple and officiant if you have the responsibility of picking the ceremony readings. There are several other translations of the Bible and each of them has a particular nuance.

You might also want to be aware that many today view some of these passages to be, shall we say, less than progressive when it comes to the status of women in today's world. Make sure you choose Bible verses compatible with your beliefs as a couple.

Remember, the Bible verses you choose can have a profound effect on the feel of the wedding. Do not take the responsibility lightly. If you are uncomfortable with scripture seek assistance from someone you trust and respect. If possible ask a minister to guide you in your scriptural search. While your choice will not make or break the ceremony, you, the couple, and the officiant should feel comfortable with the readings.

It may also be that you want secular readings in addition to, or instead of, biblical readings. You have unlimited choices in this area to assist the feel and mood of your ceremony. I advise that you pick the readings carefully and choose those that are meaningful for the two of you.

APPENDIX E
OLD TESTAMENT READINGS

Genesis 1:26–31 Creation of Man and Woman

Then God said, "Let us make man in our image, after our likeness; and let them have dominion over the fish of the sea, and over the birds of the air, and over the cattle, and over all the earth, and over every creeping thing that creeps upon the earth." So God created man in his own image, in the image of God he created him; male and female he created them. And God blessed them, and God said to them, "Be fruitful and multiply, and fill the earth and subdue it; and have dominion over the fish of the sea and over the birds of the air and over every living thing that moves upon the earth." And God said, "Behold, I have given you every plant yielding seed which is upon the face of all the earth, and every tree with seed in its fruit; you shall have them for food. And to every beast of the earth, and to every bird of the air, and to everything that creeps on the earth, everything that has the breath of life, I have given every green plant for food." And it was so. And God saw everything that he had made, and behold, it was very good. And there was evening and there was morning, a sixth day.

Genesis 2:18–25 Marriage Instituted by God

Then the Lord God said, "It is not good that the man should be alone; I will make him a helper fit for him." So out of the ground the Lord God formed every beast of the field and every bird of the air, and brought them to the man to see what he would call them; and whatever the man called every living creature, that was its name. The man gave names to all cattle, and to the birds of the air, and to every beast of the field; but for the man there was not found a helper fit for him. So the Lord God caused a deep sleep to fall upon the man, and while he slept took one of his ribs and closed up its place with flesh; and the rib which the Lord God had taken from the man he made into a woman and brought her to the man. Then the man said, "This at last is bone of my bones and flesh of my flesh; she shall be called Woman, because she was taken out of Man." Therefore a man leaves his father and his mother and cleaves to his wife, and they become one flesh. And the man and his wife were both naked, and were not ashamed.

Genesis 24:48–51, 58–67 Isaac's Marriage

Then I bowed my head and worshiped the Lord, and blessed the Lord, the God of my master Abraham, who had led me by the right way to take the daughter of my master's kinsman for his son. Now then, if you will deal loyally and truly with my master, tell me; and if not, tell me; that I may turn to the right hand or to the left." Then Laban and Bethu'el answered, "The thing comes from the Lord; we cannot speak to you bad or good. Behold, Rebekah is before you, take her and go, and let her be the wife of your master's son, as the Lord has spoken." 58: And they called Rebekah, and said to her, "Will you go with this man?" She said, "I will go." So they sent away Rebekah their sister and her nurse, and Abraham's servant and his men. And they blessed Rebekah, and said to her, "Our sister, be the mother of thousands of ten thousands; and may your descendants possess the gate of those who hate them!" Then Rebekah and her maids arose, and rode upon the camels and followed the man; thus the servant took Rebekah, and went his way. Now Isaac had come from Beer-la'hai-roi, and was dwelling in the Negeb. And Isaac went out to meditate in the field in the evening; and he lifted up his eyes and looked, and behold, there were camels coming. And Rebekah lifted up her eyes, and when she saw Isaac, she alighted from the camel, and said to the servant, "Who is the man yonder, walking in the field to meet us?" The servant said, "It is my master." So she took her veil and covered herself. And the servant told Isaac all the things that he had done. Then Isaac brought her into the tent, and took Rebekah, and she became his wife; and he loved her. So Isaac was comforted after his mother's death.

Ruth 1:16 Ruth's Love Demonstrated

But Ruth said, "Entreat me not to leave you or to return from following you; for where you go I will go, and where you lodge I will lodge; your people shall be my people, and your God my God;

Psalm 67 God Shall Govern the Earth

May God be gracious to us and bless us and make his face to shine upon us, that thy way may be known upon earth, thy saving power among all nations. Let the peoples praise thee, O God; let all the peoples praise thee! Let the nations be glad and sing for joy, for thou dost judge the peoples with equity and guide the nations upon earth. Let the peoples praise thee, O God; let all the peoples praise thee! The earth has yielded its increase; God, our God, has blessed us. God has blessed us; let all the ends of the earth fear him!

Psalm 112:1–8 Blessing of Those Who Fear God

Praise the Lord. Blessed is the man who fears the Lord, who greatly delights in his commandments! His descendants will be mighty in the land; the generation of the upright will be blessed. Wealth and riches are in his house; and his righteousness endures forever. Light rises in the darkness for the upright; the Lord is gracious, merciful, and righteous. It is well with the man who deals generously and lends, who conducts his affairs with justice. For the righteous will never be moved; he will be remembered forever. He is not afraid of evil tidings; his heart is firm, trusting in the Lord. His heart is steady, he will not be afraid, until he sees his desire on his adversaries.

Psalm 127 Children are God's Heritage

Unless the Lord builds the house, those who build it labor in vain. Unless the Lord watches over the city, the watchman stays awake in vain. It is in vain that you rise up early and go late to rest, eating the bread of anxious toil; for he gives to his beloved sleep. Lo, sons are a heritage from the Lord, the fruit of the womb a reward. Like arrows in the hand of a warrior are the sons of one's youth. Happy is the man who has his quiver full of them! He shall not be put to shame when he speaks with his enemies in the gate.

Psalm 128 Blessing on the House of the God Fearing

Blessed is every one who fears the Lord, who walks in his ways! You shall eat the fruit of the labor of your hands; you shall be happy, and it shall be well with you. Your wife will be like a fruitful vine within your house; your children will be like olive shoots around your table. Lo, thus shall the man be blessed who fears the Lord. The Lord bless you from Zion! May you see the prosperity of Jerusalem all the days of your life! May you see your children's children! Peace be upon Israel!

Psalm 134 Praise the Lord

Come, bless the Lord, all you servants of the Lord, who stand by night in the house of the Lord! Lift up your hands to the holy place, and bless the Lord! May the Lord bless you from Zion, he who made heaven and earth!

Proverbs 24:3–4 A House is Built

By wisdom a house is built, and by understanding it is established; by knowledge the rooms are filled with all precious and pleasant riches.

Proverbs 31:10–12 Wise Woman

A good wife who can find? She is far more precious than jewels. The heart of her husband trusts in her, and he will have no lack of gain. She does him good, and not harm, all the days of her life.

Song of Solomon 2:8–10, 14 Visit of King to Bride's Home

The voice of my beloved! Behold, he comes, leaping upon the mountains, bounding over the hills. My beloved is like a gazelle, or a young stag. Behold, there he stands behind our wall, gazing in at the windows, looking through the lattice. My beloved speaks and says to me: "Arise, my love, my fair one, and come away; O my dove, in the clefts of the rock, in the covert of the cliff, let me see your face, let me hear your voice, for your voice is sweet, and your face is comely.

Song of Solomon 7:10–12 Growing in Love

I am my beloved's, and his desire is for me. Come, my beloved, let us go forth into the fields, and lodge in the villages; let us go out early to the vineyards, and see whether the vines have budded, whether the grape blossoms have opened and the pomegranates are in bloom. There I will give you my love.

Song of Solomon 8:6–7 Love is as Strong as Death

Set me as a seal upon your heart, as a seal upon your arm; for love is strong as death, jealousy is cruel as the grave. Its flashes are flashes of fire, a most vehement flame. Many waters cannot quench love, neither can floods drown it. If a man offered for love all the wealth of his house, it would be utterly scorned.

Jeremiah 31:31–34 The New Covenant

"Behold, the days are coming, says the Lord, when I will make a new covenant with the house of Israel and the house of Judah, not like the covenant which I made with their fathers when I took them by the hand to bring them out of the land of Egypt, my covenant which they broke, though I was their husband, says the Lord. But this is the covenant which I will make with the house of Israel after those days, says the Lord: I will put my law within them, and I will write it upon their hearts; and I will be their God, and they shall be my people. And no longer shall each man teach his neighbor and each his brother, saying, `Know the Lord,' for they shall all know me, from the least of them to the greatest, says the Lord; for I will forgive their iniquity, and I will remember their sin no more."

APPENDIX F
NEW TESTAMENT READINGS

Matthew 5:2–12 The Beatitudes

And he opened his mouth and taught them, saying: "Blessed are the poor in spirit, for theirs is the kingdom of heaven. "Blessed are those who mourn, for they shall be comforted. "Blessed are the meek, for they shall inherit the earth. "Blessed are those who hunger and thirst for righteousness, for they shall be satisfied. "Blessed are the merciful, for they shall obtain mercy. "Blessed are the pure in heart, for they shall see God.

"Blessed are the peacemakers, for they shall be called sons of God. "Blessed are those who are persecuted for righteousness' sake, for theirs is the kingdom of heaven. "Blessed are you when men revile you and persecute you and utter all kinds of evil against you falsely on my account. Rejoice and be glad, for your reward is great in heaven, for so men persecuted the prophets who were before you.

Matthew 7:21, 24–27 House Built on Rock

"Not every one who says to me, 'Lord, Lord,' shall enter the kingdom of heaven, but he who does the will of my Father who is in heaven. "Every one then who hears these words of mine and does them will be like a wise man who built his house upon the rock; and the rain fell, and the floods came, and the winds blew and beat upon that house, but it did not fall, because it had been founded on the rock. And every one who hears these words of mine and does not do them will be like a foolish man who built his house upon the sand; and the rain fell, and the floods came, and the winds blew and beat against that house, and it fell; and great was the fall of it."

Matthew 19:4–6 Indissolubility of Marriage

He answered, "Have you not read that he who made them from the beginning made them male and female, and said, 'For this reason a man shall leave his father and mother and be joined to his wife, and the two shall become one flesh'? So they are no longer two but one flesh. What therefore God has joined together, let not man put asunder."

Matthew 22:35–40 Greatest Commandment

And one of them, a lawyer, asked him a question, to test him. "Teacher, which is the great commandment in the law?" And he said to him, "You shall love the Lord your God with all your heart, and with all your soul, and with all your mind. This is the great and first commandment. And a second is like it, You shall love your neighbor as yourself. On these two commandments depend all the law and the prophets."

Mark 10:6–9 What God Has Joined

But from the beginning of creation, `God made them male and female.' `For this reason a man shall leave his father and mother and be joined to his wife, and the two shall become one flesh.' So they are no longer two but one flesh. What therefore God has joined together, let not man put asunder."

John 2:1–11 Wedding in Cana

On the third day there was a marriage at Cana in Galilee, and the mother of Jesus was there; Jesus also was invited to the marriage, with his disciples. When the wine failed, the mother of Jesus said to him, "They have no wine." And Jesus said to her, "O woman, what have you to do with me? My hour has not yet come." His mother said to the servants, "Do whatever he tells you." Now six stone jars were standing there, for the Jewish rites of purification, each holding twenty or thirty gallons. Jesus said to them, "Fill the jars with water." And they filled them up to the brim. He said to them, "Now draw some out, and take it to the steward of the feast." So they took it. When the steward of the feast tasted the water now become wine, and did not know where it came from (though the servants who had drawn the water knew), the steward of the feast called the bridegroom and said to him, "Every man serves the good wine first; and when men have drunk freely, then the poor wine; but you have kept the good wine until now." This, the first of his signs, Jesus did at Cana in Galilee, and manifested his glory; and his disciples believed in him.

John 15:9–12 Abide in My Love

As the Father has loved me, so have I loved you; abide in my love. If you keep my commandments, you will abide in my love, just as I have kept my Father's commandments and abide in his love. These things I have spoken to you, that my joy may be in you, and that your joy may be full. "This is my commandment, that you love one another as I have loved you.

John 17:20–26 Christ Prays for All Believers

I ask not only on behalf of these, but also on behalf of those who will believe in me through their word, that they may all be one. As you, Father, are in me and I am in you, may they also be in us, so that the world may believe that you have sent me. The glory that you have given me I have given them, so that they may be one, as we are one, I in them and you in me, that they may become completely one, so that the world may know that you have sent me and have loved them even as you have loved me. Father, I desire that those also, whom you have given me, may be with me where I am, to see my glory, which you have given me because you loved me before the foundation of the world. Righteous Father, the world does not know you, but I know you; and these know that you have sent me. I made your name known to them, and I will make it known, so that the love with which you have loved me may be in them, and I in them.

Romans 8:31–35, 37–39 The Love of Christ

What then shall we say to this? If God is for us, who is against us? He who did not spare his own Son but gave him up for us all, will he not also give us all things with him? Who shall bring any charge against God's elect? It is God who justifies; who is to condemn? Is it Christ Jesus, who died, yes, who was raised from the dead, who is at the right hand of God, who indeed intercedes for us? Who shall separate us from the love of Christ? Shall tribulation, or distress, or persecution, or famine, or nakedness, or peril, or sword? No, in all these things we are more than conquerors through him who loved us. For I am sure that neither death, nor life, nor angels, nor principalities, nor things present, nor things to come, nor powers, nor height, nor depth, nor anything else in all creation, will be able to separate us from the love of God in Christ Jesus our Lord.

Roman 12:1–2, 9–12 Responsibilities Toward God

I appeal to you therefore, brethren, by the mercies of God, to present your bodies as a living sacrifice, holy and acceptable to God, which is your spiritual worship. Do not be conformed to this world but be transformed by the renewal of your mind, that you may prove what is the will of God, what is good and acceptable and perfect. 9: Let love be genuine; hate what is evil, hold fast to what is good; love one another with brotherly affection; outdo one another in showing honor. Never flag in zeal, be aglow with the Spirit, serve the Lord. Rejoice in your hope, be patient in tribulation, be constant in prayer.

1 Corinthians 6:13–15, 17–20 One Spirit with Him

"Food is meant for the stomach and the stomach for food"—and God will destroy both one and the other. The body is not meant for immorality, but for the Lord, and the Lord for the body. And God raised the Lord and will also raise us up by his power. Do you not know that your bodies are members of Christ? Shall I therefore take the members of Christ and make them members of a prostitute? Never! But he who is united to the Lord becomes one spirit with him. Shun immorality. Every other sin which a man commits is outside the body; but the immoral man sins against his own body. Do you not know that your body is a temple of the Holy Spirit within you, which you have from God? You are not your own; you were bought with a price. So glorify God in your body.

1 Corinthians 13:1–8, 13 The Love Chapter (NOTE: May already be used in the service)

If I speak in the tongues of men and of angels, but have not love, I am a noisy gong or a clanging cymbal. And if I have prophetic powers, and understand all mysteries and all knowledge, and if I have all faith, so as to remove mountains, but have not love, I am nothing. If I give away all I have, and if I deliver my body to be burned, but have not love, I gain nothing. Love is patient and kind; love is not jealous or boastful; it is not arrogant or rude. Love does not insist on its own way; it is not irritable or resentful; it does not rejoice at wrong, but rejoices in the right. Love bears all things, believes all things, hopes all things, endures all things. Love never ends; as for prophecies, they will pass away; as for tongues, they will cease; as for knowledge, it will pass away. So faith, hope, love abide, these three; but the greatest of these is love.

Ephesians 3:14–21 The Love of Christ

For this reason I bow my knees before the Father, from whom every family in heaven and on earth is named, that according to the riches of his glory he may grant you to be strengthened with might through his Spirit in the inner man, and that Christ may dwell in your hearts through faith; that you, being rooted and grounded in love, may have power to comprehend with all the saints what is the breadth and length and height and depth, and to know the love of Christ which surpasses knowledge, that you may be filled with all the fullness of God. Now to him who by the power at work within us is able to do far more abundantly than all that we ask or think, to him be glory in the church and in Christ Jesus to all generations, for ever and ever. Amen.

Ephesians 5:20–33 Mystery of Marriage

Always and for everything giving thanks in the name of our Lord Jesus Christ to God the Father. Be subject to one another out of reverence for Christ. Wives, be subject to your husbands, as to the Lord. For the husband is the head of the wife as Christ is the head of the church, his body, and is himself its Savior. As the church is subject to Christ, so let wives also be subject in everything to their husbands. Husbands, love your wives, as Christ loved the church and gave himself up for her, that he might sanctify her, having cleansed her by the washing of water with the word, that he might present the church to himself in splendor, without spot or wrinkle or any such thing, that she might be holy and without blemish. Even so husbands should love their wives as their own bodies. He who loves his wife loves himself. For no man ever hates his own flesh, but nourishes and cherishes it, as Christ does the church, because we are members of his body. "For this reason a man shall leave his father and mother and be joined to his wife, and the two shall become one flesh." This mystery is a profound one, and I am saying that it refers to Christ and the church; however, let each one of you love his wife as himself, and let the wife see that she respects her husband.

Colossians 3:12–17 Love and Thanksgiving

Put on then, as God's chosen ones, holy and beloved, compassion, kindness, lowliness, meekness, and patience, forbearing one another and, if one has a complaint against another, forgiving each other; as the Lord has forgiven you, so you also must forgive. And above all these put on love, which binds everything together in perfect harmony. And let the peace of Christ rule in your hearts, to which indeed you were called in the one body. And be thankful. Let the word of Christ dwell in you richly, teach and admonish one another in all wisdom, and sing psalms and hymns and spiritual songs with thankfulness in your hearts to

God. And whatever you do, in word or deed, do everything in the name of the Lord Jesus, giving thanks to God the Father through him.

1 Peter 3:1–9 Submission in Marriage

Likewise you wives, be submissive to your husbands, so that some, though they do not obey the word, may be won without a word by the behavior of their wives, when they see your reverent and chaste behavior. Let not yours be the outward adorning with braiding of hair, decoration of gold, and wearing of fine clothing, but let it be the hidden person of the heart with the imperishable jewel of a gentle and quiet spirit, which in God's sight is very precious. So once the holy women who hoped in God used to adorn themselves and were submissive to their husbands, as Sarah obeyed Abraham, calling him lord. And you are now her children if you do right and let nothing terrify you. Likewise you husbands, live considerately with your wives, bestowing honor on the woman as the weaker sex, since you are joint heirs of the grace of life, in order that your prayers may not be hindered. Finally, all of you, have unity of spirit, sympathy, love of the brethren, a tender heart and a humble mind. Do not return evil for evil or reviling for reviling; but on the contrary bless, for to this you have been called, that you may obtain a blessing.

1 John 3:18–24 Love in Deed and Truth

Little children, let us not love in word or speech but in deed and in truth. By this we shall know that we are of the truth, and reassure our hearts before him whenever our hearts condemn us; for God is greater than our hearts, and he knows everything. Beloved, if our hearts do not condemn us, we have confidence before God; and we receive from him whatever we ask, because we keep his commandments and do what pleases him. And this is his commandment, that we should believe in the name of his Son Jesus Christ and love one another, just as he has commanded us. All who keep his commandments abide in him, and he in them. And by this we know that he abides in us, by the Spirit which he has given us.

1 John 4:7–19 Love is of God

Beloved, let us love one another; for love is of God, and he who loves is born of God and knows God. He who does not love does not know God; for God is love. In this the love of God was made manifest among us, that God sent his only Son into the world, so that we might live through him. In this is love, not that we loved God but that he loved us and sent his Son to be the expiation for our sins. Beloved, if God so loved us, we also ought to love one another. No man has ever seen God; if we love one another, God abides in us and his love is perfected in us. By this we know that we abide in him and he in us, because he has given us of his own Spirit. And we have seen and testify that the Father has sent his Son as the Savior of the world. Whoever confesses that Jesus is the Son of God, God abides in him, and he in God. So we know and believe the love God has for us. God is love, and he who abides in love abides in God, and God abides in him. In this is love perfected with us, that we may have confidence for the day of judgment, because as he is so are we in this world. There is no fear in love, but perfect love casts out fear. For fear has to do with punishment, and he who fears is not perfected in love. We love, because he first loved us.

Revelation 19:1, 5–9 Marriage Supper of the Lamb

After this I heard what seemed to be the loud voice of a great multitude in heaven, crying, "Hallelujah! Salvation and glory and power belong to our God, And from the throne came a voice crying, "Praise our God, all you his servants, you who fear him, small and great." Then I heard what seemed to be the voice of a great multitude, like the sound of many waters and like the sound of mighty thunderpeals, crying, "Hallelujah! For the Lord our God the Almighty reigns. Let us rejoice and exult and give him the glory, for the marriage of the Lamb has come, and his Bride has made herself ready; it was granted her to be clothed with fine linen, bright and pure"—for the fine linen is the righteous deeds of the saints. And the angel said to me, "Write this: Blessed are those who are invited to the marriage supper of the Lamb." And he said to me, "These are true words of God."

ABOUT THE AUTHOR

Rev. Dr. Russell K. Elleven earned the bachelor's degree from Texas Christian University, the master's degree from the Divinity School of Vanderbilt University, and the doctorate in Education and Counseling from the University of North Texas. He is duly ordained to perform wedding ceremonies in the state of Texas, Hawaii, and elsewhere and has presided over hundreds of ceremonies. He has published on a variety of topics, has conducted seminars nationally, and is a licensed counselor. The greatest day of his life was June 30, 1992, when he married Gayle.

If you have suggestions for future editions of this book you may contact the author through either of his webpages (http://www.marriage-education.net or http://www.wedding-ceremony.com) both of which receive thousands of hits each month.

ORDER THIS BOOK FOR OTHERS

Reverent Rituals:
A Brief Wedding Guide

Congratulations on your engagement!

In this little book couples will find many suggestions for their wedding. Where will you marry? Who will officiate? What will the ceremony be like? Does everything have to be so stressful?

The answers to these questions and more will be found in this book. Couples will find a variety of tips to make their wedding planning easier and more complete. Rev. Elleven answers questions that many couples do not even know to ask.

Written by an ordained minister and licensed counselor in an abbreviated manner, this guide allows couples to put ideas into action quickly and easily. After finishing *Reverent Rituals: A Brief Wedding Guide* couples will be well on their way to planning the best wedding possible.

—

Rev. Dr. Russell K. Elleven earned a bachelor's degree from Texas Christian University, a master's degree from the Divinity School of Vanderbilt University, and a doctorate in Education and Counseling from the University of North Texas. He is an ordained minister and licensed counselor and has presided over hundreds of ceremonies.

ORDER THIS BOOK FOR OTHERS

You can give *Reverent Rituals: A Brief Wedding Guide* to friends or family members who are getting married. Just follow these simple steps:

1. Point your web browser to http://www.wedding-ceremony.com

2. Click on the book cover icon

3. Follow those easy, step-by-step instructions on your screen

Thanks for your support!

0-595-29807-9